BREAKING THE CODE

BREAKING THE CODE

Understanding the Book of Revelation

BRUCE M. METZGER

Abingdon Press
Nashville

BREAKING THE CODE
Understanding the Book of Revelation

Copyright © 1993 by Abingdon Press

Leader's Guide prepared by Donn Downall

This book is printed on acid-free paper.

Scripture quotations in this publication, unless otherwise indicated, are from the New Revised Standard Version Bible, copyright © 1989 by the Division of Christian Education of the National Council of the Churches of Christ in the USA. Used by permission.

Those noted RSV are from the Revised Standard Version of the Bible, copyright 1946, 1952, 1971 by the Division of Christian Education of the National Council of the Churches of Christ in the USA. Used by permission.

Map of Asia Minor on page 20 is reproduced by permission of Thomas Nelson and Sons Ltd., Walton-on-Thames, Surrey, England.

Cover art: *The Four Horsemen of the Apocalypse,* woodcut by Albrecht Dürer (A.D. 1498).

Library of Congress Cataloging-in-Publication Data

Metzger, Bruce Manning.
    Breaking the code: understanding the book of Revelation / Bruce M. Metzger
    p. cm.
    Includes bibliographical references and index.
    ISBN 0-687-08999-9 (alk. paper)
    1. Bible. N.T. Revelation—Criticism, interpretation, etc.
I. Title.
BS2825.2.M49   1993
228'.06—dc20

93-5954
CIP

99 00 01 02 03 04 05 06 07 — 20 19 18 17 16 15 14 13

MANUFACTURED IN THE UNITED STATES OF AMERICA

To Isobel Mackay Metzger

CONTENTS

PREFACE

F OR most church members, the book of Revelation is a closed book. They avoid it, thinking it too mysterious for them to understand. On the other hand, a few people seem to live in the book of Revelation, concentrating all their reading of Scripture on this one book alone. Both of these extremes are shortsighted and ill-advised.

The book of Revelation contains passages of great beauty and comfort that have sustained Christian believers over the ages. Doubtless there are parts that seem to the casual reader to be bizarre and bewildering. But when one approaches the book recognizing that it belongs to a special type of literature (the apocalyptic type), then one can begin to appreciate the overall message of John, the theologian of Patmos. Of course, some parts will remain enigmatic, but on the whole the attentive reader will be surprised to find how much of the book makes sense.

For a good many years the present writer has had an academic as well as a personal interest in the book of Revelation. The task of giving lectures on Revelation to theological students as well as presenting Bible studies of this book to church people in various congregations has required both a scholarly and a devotional consideration of this remarkable book.

The approach of the present volume has in mind the needs

and interests of the general nontheological reader. Special attention is directed to the literary form and the spiritual message of Revelation. Footnotes are kept to a minimum, and the application is more than once directed to present-day realities of the Christian life.

Quotations of Scripture are made from the New Revised Standard Version of the Bible. In the exposition of the text occasional phrases have been adapted from the present writer's comments on Revelation in *The New Oxford Annotated Bible* (New York: Oxford University Press, 1991).

In conclusion, I must thank many who have contributed to whatever insights into the meaning of Revelation may be contained in the following pages. Questions from both students and church members, as well as information gleaned from a broad range of commentaries, have helped to bring these chapters to a focus. It is hoped that the first steps undertaken here will kindle in readers a new appreciation for the book of Revelation, leading to further study of its pages.

The volume is dedicated to my wife, Isobel Mackay Metzger, without whose help and encouragement it would not have been written.

Bruce M. Metzger
Princeton Theological Seminary
Princeton, New Jersey

1

INTRODUCING THE BOOK OF REVELATION

THE entire Bible is a library, containing different types of books. Now different types of literature make their appeal to the reader through different avenues. For example, the Psalms of David touch one's *emotions*: "Bless the LORD, O my soul, and all that is within me, bless his holy name" (Ps. 103:1). In the Bible are also books of law that involve commands: "Do this!" "Don't do that!" Such books speak to our *will*, requiring us to respond positively or negatively. Still other biblical writings, such as Paul's Letter to the Romans, appeal primarily to our *intellect*. We need to think carefully and patiently as we seek to follow the apostle's theological reasoning.

The book of Revelation is unique in appealing primarily to our *imagination*—not, however, a freewheeling imagination, but a disciplined imagination. This book contains a series of word pictures, as though a number of slides were being shown upon a great screen. As we watch we allow ourselves to be carried along by impressions created by these pictures. Many of the details of the pictures are intended to contribute to the total impression, and are not to be isolated and interpreted with wooden literalism.

PRELIMINARY CONSIDERATIONS

In order to become oriented to the book of Revelation one must take seriously what the author says happened. John tells us that he had a series of visions. He says that he "heard" certain words and "saw" certain visions. Over the centuries there have been occasional individuals with the gift of being susceptible to visionary experiences. The author of Revelation seems to have been such a person.

In order to understand what is involved in a visionary experience we may consider Ezekiel's vision of a valley full of dry bones (Ezek. 37:1-4). In this vision the prophet saw the assembling of the bones into skeletons and the coming of sinews and flesh, climaxed by restoration to life, so that "they lived, and stood on their feet, a vast multitude" (Ezek. 37:10). We are not to understand that bones were actually scattered around in a valley; the account is purely symbolic. The prophet's visionary experience pictured the revival of the dead nation of Israel, hopelessly scattered in exile. Through this vision Ezekiel was assured that the dispersed Israelites, living as exiles in foreign lands, would be re-established as a nation in their own land.

The Acts of the Apostles reports several instances of visionary experiences (9:10; 10:11; 16:9; 18:9; 22:17; cf. 27:23). One of the most significant was the apostle Peter's experience at the house of Simon, a tanner, in Joppa. In this case a natural cause cooperated in producing the vision. Hungry, and waiting for a meal to be prepared, Peter fell into a trance and saw "something like a large sheet coming down, being lowered to the ground by its four corners" (Acts 10:11). In it were all kinds of quadrupeds, reptiles, and birds, both fit and unfit for food according to Jewish law and custom. The vision was accompanied by a heavenly voice bidding Peter to slaughter and eat what was provided (Acts 10:13). This vision taught Peter that, as a Jewish Christian, he need no longer restrict his diet to kosher foods only, but was permitted to visit and even to reside at the home of Gentiles.[1] We are not to think that there was literally a sheet filled with various creatures.

Similarly, when the book of Revelation reports that John "saw a beast rising out of the sea, having ten horns and seven heads" (13:1), there is no reason to imagine that such a creature actually existed. Nevertheless, the vision had profound significance for John—and still has for the reader today (see pp. 75-77 below). Such accounts combine cognitive insight with emotional response. They invite the reader or listener to enter into the experience being recounted and to participate in it, triggering mental images of that which is described.

JOHN'S SYMBOLIC LANGUAGE

In reporting his visionary experiences John frequently uses symbolic language. Sometimes he explains the meaning of the symbols. Other symbols really need no explanation; for example, the number *seven*. Everyone knows that there are seven days in a week; then another week begins. And so seven means completion or perfection. Other symbols in Revelation can be understood in the light of the symbolism used in the Hebrew Scriptures, particularly the books of Ezekiel, Daniel, and Zechariah. It is clear that John had studied the Old Testament very thoroughly. Of the 404 verses that comprise the 22 chapters of the book of Revelation, 278 verses contain one or more allusions to an Old Testament passage. John had so thoroughly pondered the Old Testament that when it came to recording the import of his visions of God and of heaven, he expressed himself by using phrases borrowed from the prophets of Israel. Therefore, in attempting to understand John's symbolism, we must consider not only the book itself, but also his use of the Old Testament.

---

1. Because of the vision, Peter agreed to go to the home of the Roman centurion, Cornelius, where he stayed for several days preaching to Gentiles (Acts 10:22-48).

No doubt some of John's symbols seem exceedingly strange to readers today. For example, the Roman Empire is symbolized as a beast like a leopard with feet like a bear's and a mouth like a lion's mouth (13:2)—all very horrible indeed, as those who were being persecuted by Rome knew well. Such strange beasts were more or less commonplace features in apocalyptic literature—and the book of Revelation is a notable example of that literary genre. More will be said later about such literature, but for the moment it is sufficient to remind ourselves that we too make use of animals as symbols of nations and groups: the British lion, the Russian bear, the American eagle, the Democratic donkey, the Republican elephant. A newspaper cartoonist may show a donkey tugging at one end of a rope and an elephant tugging at the other. Young children or new immigrants may not understand that symbolism. Later, they will recognize the competition within a two-party system. In the same way, some of the imagery in Revelation may seem unusual or even bizarre, but on further reflection, and with the use of a disciplined imagination, the meaning will usually become clear. In any case, it is important to recognize that the descriptions are *descriptions of symbols, not of the reality conveyed by the symbols.*

IDENTITY OF THE AUTHOR

The author four times calls himself "John" (1:1, 4, 9; 22:8). This name was common among Jews from the time of the Exile onward and among the early Christians. Four persons are mentioned in the New Testament who bore this name. Which of these is intended, or whether the author was some other early Christian leader with this name, has been extensively debated. The absence of any specific data in the book itself makes it difficult to come to a firm decision. Since there is no qualifying identification (such as "John the elder" or "John Mark"), it is probable that the author intends his readers to understand that he is the John, who was so well known that he needed no titles or credentials. Certainly from the mid-second century onward the book was widely, though not universally, ascribed to the apostle John, the son of Zebedee. This attribution was accepted in the West beginning with Justin Martyr of Rome (A.D. 150), Irenaeus of Gaul (180), and Tertullian of North Africa (200).

In the East, however, apostolic authorship was sometimes rejected, notably by the so-called Alogi (a group of heretics in Asia Minor, about A.D. 170), as well as by Dionysius, bishop of Alexandria (after 247). Dionysius argued on the basis of differences of vocabulary and grammatical style between the Fourth Gospel and the Apocalypse and believed the latter to be the work of another person named John, who, however, he was prepared to say, was "holy and inspired."[2]

From this point on, the apostolic origin of Revelation was frequently disputed in the East. Eusebius (A.D. 325) wavered between regarding the book as "recognized" or as "spurious." But after Athanasius of Alexandria (A.D. 367) and the Latin church under the influence of Augustine toward the end of the fourth century had accepted Revelation in their lists of the canon, the book was no longer officially contested as part of the New Testament. Even though the precise identity of "John" is still debated today, interpretation of the book does not depend on certainty concerning this matter.

TIME OF WRITING OF REVELATION

The book of Revelation was composed and sent to seven churches in the Roman province of Asia at some point between A.D. 69 and 96 in order to encourage them with the assurance that, despite all the forces marshalled against them, victory was theirs if they remained loyal to Christ. Although some scholars have identified the persecutions alluded to in the book as originating from the Emperor Nero (A.D. 54–68),

---

2. Reported by Eusebius in his *Church History* V. xxv. 7.

it is more likely that the book reflects the conditions prevailing during the latter years of the Emperor Domitian (A.D. 81–96).

Prior to Domitian the state religion had not discriminated against the Christian faith. Nero's mad acts against Christians were restricted to Rome (see pp. 85-86 below) and had nothing to do with the issue of worship. The first emperor who tried to compel Christians to participate in Caesar worship was Domitian. Toward the close of his reign he became so overweeningly proud and arrogant that he demanded people address him as "our lord and god" (*dominus et deus noster* in Latin). Of course, faithful Christians would not address any human being as lord and god or participate in offering incense to him in temples built in his honor. The Jews had earlier been granted immunity from such requirements, and could legally abstain from pagan worship. At first the Roman authorities regarded the Christians as a sect within Judaism. But toward the close of the first century it became clear that the church was separate from the synagogue; therefore, Christians who refused to participate in emperor worship exposed themselves to the charge not only of being unpatriotic, but also of being subversive and enemies of the state. Consequently, at various times and places they suffered persecution because of their faith.

Also favoring the close of the first century as the time of the composition of Revelation is the fact that, according to 2:8-11, the church in Smyrna had been persevering under trials for a long time, whereas according to Polycarp,[3] the bishop of Smyrna in the first half of the second century, the church there did not yet exist until after the time of Paul (that is, in the 60s). Furthermore, in 3:17 the church in Laodicea is described as rich, though this city had been almost completely destroyed by an earthquake in A.D. 61 (see p. 43 below).

One may conclude, therefore, that the book of Revelation was written toward the end of Domitian's reign, about A.D.

---

3. His *Letter to the Philippians,* 11.3.

90–95. This date is corroborated by the testimony of early church fathers, such as Irenaeus (A.D. 180), Clement of Alexandria (200), Origen (254), and Eusebius (325).

LITERARY GENRE OF THE BOOK

John called his book an "Apocalypse," meaning an unveiling, a disclosure. This alerts us at once to pay attention to the special characteristics of this book, so different from other types of literature. During the two centuries before and after Christ a considerable number of Jewish and Christian writings appeared that belong to the category of apocalyptic literature. Jewish apocalyptic literature begins with the book of Daniel, though apocalyptic tendencies can be seen in Isaiah 24–27, Ezekiel 38–39, and Zechariah 9–14, where there are frequent references to the approaching "day of the LORD."

Important apocalyptic writings outside the Old Testament are the book of Enoch, the Apocalypse of Baruch, the Fourth Book of Ezra, the Ascension of Isaiah, the Apocalypse of Zephaniah, and parts of the Sibylline Oracles.[4] The apocalyptists receive their revelations in ecstatic or dream visions, which are reported with the stylistic features typical of apocalyptic literature. Persons are represented in the likeness of animals, and historical events in the form of natural phenomena. Colors and numbers have secret meanings. The images themselves often have a history behind them and originate from astrological, cosmological, and mythological tradition of antiquity.

Although there are no formal laws that are applicable to all apocalypses, most of these books have the following basic features:

1. The authors of such books view the universe as divided into two camps, one good and the other evil. These camps are

---

4.   An English translation of these and other apocalyptic books is available in *The Old Testament Pseudepigrapha*, vol. I, *Apocalyptic Literature and Testaments*, ed. James H. Charlesworth (Garden City, N.Y.: Doubleday, 1983).

engaged in a long and fearful struggle. Behind the conflict are supernatural powers (God and Satan) at work among people and institutions. In everyday life it is not always easy to distinguish clearly the works of the two, but at the end of time every human being will be found to be on one side or the other. The final separation of the two is the meaning of judgment.

2. Apocalypses usually contain predictions about the final outcome of human affairs, focusing on the last age of the world, when good will triumph and evil will be judged. Present troubles are represented as "birth pangs" that will usher in the End. God has set a limit to the era of wickedness and will intervene at the appointed time to execute judgment. In the final battle the powers of evil, together with the evil nations they represent, will be utterly destroyed. Then a new order will be established, when the End will be as the Beginning, and Paradise will be restored.

OUTLINE OF THE BOOK

The focus of the book of Revelation is the Second Coming of the Lord Jesus Christ and the definitive establishment of God's kingdom at the end of time. Corresponding to this, the structure of the book involves a series of parallel yet ever-progressing sections. These bring before the reader, over and over again, but in climacteric form, the struggle of the church and its victory over the world in the providence of God. There are probably seven[5] of these sections, though only five are clearly marked. The plan of the whole, then, can be divided as follows: Prologue (1:1-8); seven parallel sections

---

5. John is fond of sevens; he mentions seven golden lampstands, seven stars, seven flaming torches, seven spirits of God, seven eyes, seven seals, seven angels, seven trumpets, seven thunders, seven heads on the dragon, seven plagues, seven bowls, seven mountains, and seven kings. Furthermore, without directly enumerating them, John includes seven beatitudes scattered throughout his book (see p. 22, note 1 below) as well as the seven-fold praise presented to the Lamb (5:12).

divided at 3:22; 8:2; 11:19; 14:20; 16:21; and 19:21; Epilogue (22:6-21).

Here and there in John's account of his visionary experiences he uses the word *then*. There is, however, no reason to assume that the order in which John received his visions must be the order in which the contents of the visions are to be fulfilled. In chapter 12, for example, we will find a vision that takes us back to the time of the birth of Jesus. Such features in the book should make us wary of turning Revelation into a kind of almanac or time chart of the last days based on the sequence of the visions that John experienced. Like any good teacher, he knows that repetition is a helpful learning device, and so he repeats his messages more than once from differing points of view.

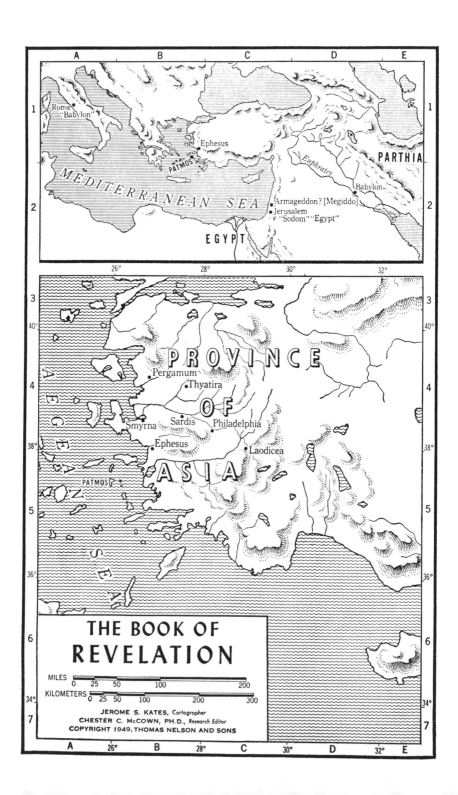

THE BOOK OF
REVELATION

MILES
0 25 50   100   200

KILOMETERS
0 25 50 100   200   300

JEROME S. KATES, *Cartographer*
CHESTER C. McCOWN, PH.D., *Research Editor*
COPYRIGHT 1949, THOMAS NELSON AND SONS

2

JOHN'S VISION OF THE HEAVENLY CHRIST

(Revelation 1:1-20)

THE PROLOGUE (1:1-3)

In the opening sentence of the prologue John discloses to the reader the origin and content of his book: "The revelation of Jesus Christ, which God gave him to show his servants what must soon take place; he made it known by sending his angel to his servant John" (1:1). The source of the revelation is God, who speaks through the Son, who shows to God's people the things that are to be. This revelation is the revelation "of Jesus Christ," which can mean either that the revelation was made by Jesus Christ or that it was made about him or that it belongs to him. In a sense all three are true: the revelation comes from God through Jesus Christ, who communicates it to John by an angel. The revelation is Jesus Christ's and the chain of communication is God—Jesus Christ—angel—John—to the churches. The purpose of the revelation is to show "what must soon take place." Here the sense of "must" is not the necessity imposed by Fate, but the sure fulfillment of the purpose of God. The word *soon* indicates that John intended his message for his own generation.

The material in the book of Revelation is so important that a blessing[1] is promised to the one who reads it aloud, and to those who hear and who keep what is written in the prophecy (1:3). The word *aloud* is not in the Greek, but is implied. In New Testament times reading was usually a group activity, with one person reading to others. Not all people, of course, could read; furthermore, manuscripts of books were expensive, and few Christians could afford them. In the absence of printed books, great emphasis was laid in the early church on the public reading of handwritten copies of communications to congregations (Col. 4:16; 1 Thess. 5:27; cf. 1 Tim. 4:13). John calls his book *prophecy*; it has the weight of the words of the prophets of the Old Testament. For this reason, therefore, a divine blessing can be pronounced on those who read and who hear the book.

THE SALUTATION: GREETINGS TO THE CHURCHES
(REVELATION 1:4-8)

The practical character of the prophetic word (1:3) is implied by the personal greetings that the writer extends to the recipients of his book. The immediate recipients are "the seven churches that are in Asia" (1:4). The salutation thus indicates that the entire book, and not merely the portion containing the seven letters (chapters 2 and 3), is intended for the churches of Asia. This "Asia" does not refer to the great continent of that name, but to the Roman province of Asia, located in the western part of what we call Asia Minor. We do not know on what principle the seven churches were selected. There were certainly more than seven churches in the region by the time this book was written (Acts 20:5ff.; Col. 1:2; 4:13). John may have had a special relationship with these seven. In any case, seven is a number symbolizing completeness. The

---

1. There are seven beatitudes scattered through the book of Revelation. The other six are at 14:13; 16:15; 19:9; 20:6; 22:7 and 14.

particular churches addressed were, therefore, representative of the whole church in all the world.

John opens his communication with a dual salutation, "Grace and peace." The apostle Paul had used this salutation at the beginning of all his letters, and it soon became a traditional greeting among Christians (compare also 1 and 2 Peter 1:2). The salutation invokes the grace and peace (the two always stand in this order, never peace and grace) that come from God, and reminds us of the favor and acceptance that God has extended to believers. And it is because of God's grace that his people can enjoy peace—peace with God as well as the peace of God, resulting in inner poise and tranquility, even amid the hardest experiences of life.

To this dual salutation John adds three phrases identifying the source of the grace and peace. They come, he says, "from him who is and who was and who is to come, and from the seven spirits who are before his throne, and from Jesus Christ" (1:4). We see here an allusion to the three Persons of the Godhead, though they are arranged in an unaccustomed order, and the manner of referring to the Holy Spirit is unusual. Perhaps we would have been inclined to say that God is the one who was, and is, and is to be, but John wishes to stress the eternal presence of God and so he begins by referring to the one who "is." This is the primary thing to say about God: God is the ever-present one. Here John may be alluding to the self-disclosure of God to Moses, "I AM WHO I AM" (Exod. 3:14).

Grace and peace, John continues, also come "from the seven spirits who are before the throne." Although some have taken this to refer to seven created angels, it is more likely that John uses the expression in order to symbolize the plenitude and power of the Holy Spirit. The idea seems to arise from Isaiah 11:2 in the Greek translation of the Old Testament (the Septuagint) where seven designations of the spirit of the Lord are mentioned: "the spirit of wisdom and understanding, the spirit of counsel and might, the spirit of knowledge and godliness, the spirit of the fear of God."

Grace and peace are also from Jesus Christ, who is described as "the faithful witness, the firstborn of the dead, and the ruler of the kings of the earth" (1:5). In a day when many were suffering because of their Christian witness, it would encourage them to be reminded that Jesus Christ was "the faithful witness" *par excellence* (see 1 Tim. 6:13). The following description, "the firstborn of the dead, and the ruler of the kings of the earth," is an echo of Psalm 89:27, where God appoints David (and, by implication, the son of David) "the firstborn, the highest of the kings of the earth." Here John's use of the title "the firstborn" is related to Christ's status in resurrection, as in Colossians 1:18 (cf. 1 Cor. 15:20; also Rom. 8:29).

But why does John list the three in the order of God, Spirit, and Jesus Christ? The answer is simple: John intends to continue his reference to Jesus Christ by the addition of a doxology and other statements about Christ, and so, instead of interrupting the sequence of subjects (God—Jesus—Spirit— and Jesus once again), he varies the accustomed order so as to provide a smoother transition to the doxology. John's further description of Jesus Christ identifies him as the one "who loves us and freed us from our sins by his blood" (1:5). The choice of tenses of the verbs is noteworthy. Jesus Christ, he says, loves us right now in the present, and in the past he freed us from our sin when he died on the cross. Some of the later Greek manuscripts read, "who loves us and washed us from our sins," where the scribes confused the word *lusanti* ("freed") with the word *lousanti* ("washed"). Actually both readings are theologically significant: believers have been freed from the chain of sin as well as cleansed from the stain of sin.

The act of Christ's setting us free from our sins was followed by his making us to be "a kingdom, priests serving his God and Father" (1:6). This is the truth that Protestant Reformers emphasized in the doctrine of the universal priesthood of all believers. Through Jesus Christ every Christian has access to God and can intercede on behalf of others.

The solemn opening of the book reaches its climax with words ascribed to the Lord God: "I am the Alpha and the Omega" (1:8). These are the first and last letters of the Greek alphabet, and suggest that God is first and last, an idea that was earlier expressed by Isaiah (44:6), implying that God was before all things and will outlast all things. God's eternity is brought out once again by the addition of the statement, "who is and who was and who is to come, the Almighty." At this point the introductory paragraphs come to a close.

JOHN'S FIRST VISION
(REVELATION 1:9-20)

John introduces his first vision by telling his readers that he was on the island of Patmos because he had proclaimed God's message and the truth that Jesus revealed (1:9-10). Patmos is a rocky, mountainous island, about ten miles long and six miles wide, some thirty miles west of Asia Minor in the Aegean Sea. The Romans used it as a place of political banishment.

How long John had been on Patmos we do not know, but he tells us that on a certain Lord's day he fell into a trance and was caught up in the spirit. A trumpet-like voice behind him said, "Write[2] in a book what you see and send it to the seven churches, to Ephesus, to Smyrna, to Pergamum, to Thyatira, to Sardis, to Philadelphia, and to Laodicea" (1:11).

Why do the names of the churches stand in their present order? Some have suggested that the messages sent to them depict successively the status of the church at important stages down through the ages. But there is not the slightest indica-

---

2. Whether the seer had writing materials on Patmos and was able to write the book while in exile, or whether this could be done only after the death of Domitian (A.D. 96) when John returned once again to Ephesus, is not known.

tion in the text that this is so. The reason for the present order is much more simple: it is the order in which, starting from Ephesus (the city closest to Patmos), a messenger carrying the book would travel, somewhat in a semicircle, going successively to each of the churches. The average distance between each locality is between twenty-five and fifty miles. A glance at a map (see p. 20) will show that the seven cities are so situated as to be centers from which the book could be circulated through a very wide expanse of country.

Having heard the trumpet-like voice behind him, John turned and beheld the heavenly Christ in majestic, breathtaking splendor. This is how he describes his vision:

> I saw seven golden lampstands,[3] and in the midst of the lampstands I saw one like the Son of Man, clothed with a long robe and with a golden sash across his chest. His head and his hair were white as white wool, white as snow; his eyes were like a flame of fire, his feet were like burnished bronze, refined as in a furnace, and his voice was like the sound of many waters. In his right hand he held seven stars, and from his mouth came a sharp, two-edged sword, and his face was like the sun shining with full force. (1:12-16)

How shall we understand this description of the heavenly Christ? It may seem paradoxical to say that the description does not mean what it says; it means what it means. We note first that the writer explains part of the symbolism at the end of the chapter: "the seven lampstands are the seven churches" (1:20). Therefore when John says he saw Christ in the midst of the lampstands, he wants to let us know that Christ is not an absentee landlord. On the contrary, he is in the midst of his churches, supporting them during trials and persecutions. Furthermore, when John describes Christ as wearing a long

---

3. The rendering "candlesticks" in some English versions is a mistake in translation; candles were not invented until the Middle Ages.

robe with a golden sash across his chest, we should ask ourselves who wore that kind of clothing. The answer is that kings wore such garments, and that this is John's way of referring to Christ as king.

When we read that Christ has hair like white wool, white as snow, John does not mean that the Lord is prematurely aged. This description is taken from a passage in Daniel (7:9) where the prophet describes his vision of God, the Ancient of Days. In this way John assigns a dignity to Christ in terms that resemble Daniel's vision of God Almighty. Piercing eyes "like a flame of fire" burn away our shams and hypocrisies, looking into our innermost selves. "Feet like burnished bronze" represent strength and stability (contrast Dan. 2:33, 41). John describes the voice of Christ as penetrating and unmistakable, "like the sound of many waters," words that the prophet Ezekiel used to describe the God of Israel (Ezek. 43:2). The meaning of the seven stars that Christ holds in his right hand is explained at the end of the chapter; they "are the angels of the seven churches" (1:20). The sword that comes from his mouth symbolizes his word of judgment (see Heb. 4:12). Finally, John says that the face of Christ is like the sun shining with full strength. What a magnificent climax to an exalted vision!

Instead of taking John's account with flat-footed literalism, we should imaginatively allow ourselves to be guided by the poetic quality of the narrative. We trivialize the account if we make a composite picture of the heavenly Christ showing each of these features literalistically. One should think of it like this: a young man writes a love letter to his fiancée, describing how charming she is. Her eyes, he says, are like limpid pools of water, her cheeks are like rose petals, and her neck is graceful, like the neck of a swan. If someone were to draw a picture, literalistically depicting all these features, the young woman certainly would not feel flattered! So too, John's description of the heavenly Christ does not mean what it says; it means what it means.

In the presence of such a sublime and wonderful experience, John is overcome with awe, and he falls down "as though dead" (1:17). But he is quickly made to stand up again by the touch of Christ's right hand—for the whole point of the vision is not to overwhelm John, but to reassure him by showing Christ resplendent with divine attributes. After bidding John not to be afraid, Christ identifies himself, saying, "I am the first and the last, and the living one. I was dead, and see, I am alive forever and ever; and I have the keys of Death and of Hades" (1:17-18). In these three statements the seer is assured that the heavenly Christ bears the same titles as does the Lord God, the Almighty (see verse 8), and that after Jesus had conquered death, he is preeminently "the living one . . . alive forever and ever." To "have the keys of Death and of Hades" is to possess authority over their domain. No distinction is to be drawn here between Death and Hades; they combine to express one idea, the realm of the departed. Because Christ has the "keys," the time and manner of the death of each person are under his control. Therefore his people, who were sometimes threatened with death because of their loyalty to him, need not fear that death will separate them from his love.

At the conclusion of the vision, John receives the command to write "what you have seen, what is, and what is to take place after this" (1:19). What John has seen embraced both the situation already in existence and things that still lay in the future. One of the chief problems in the interpretation of the book of Revelation is to distinguish between those elements in John's visions that symbolize "what is" from those that symbolize "what is to take place after this" (1:19).

3

LETTERS TO CHURCHES

(Revelation 2:1-29)

U NLIKE John's vision of the heavenly Christ in chapter 1, the setting of chapters 2 and 3 is on earth. These two chapters present the messages that Christ directs to each of seven churches in the Roman province of Asia, located in the western part of Asia Minor. By the 90s of the first century there were many more than seven churches in western Asia Minor. Besides those mentioned here, we know from Paul's letters the names of several other cities in which there were Christian congregations. Why, we may ask, were no messages written to them? It may be, of course, that John was acquainted with just these seven. On the other hand, since seven is a very special number, meaning complete, all-inclusive, it appears that, by identifying just seven churches, John wishes to suggest that the messages are intended for all churches, wherever they may be located.

The literary structure of the seven letters[1] discloses a certain uniform pattern. Each message is prefaced with an identification of the heavenly Christ. John uses one or another of the

---

1. The messages to the seven churches have been traditionally called "letters," but there is no evidence that these portions of chapters 2 and 3 originated as separate documents. All Greek manuscripts of the book of Revelation incorporate all of them, and none of the seven exists by itself.

various features from the symbolic description of Christ that he gave in chapter 1. Thus, the first letter is introduced by the statement, " These are the words of him who holds the seven stars in his right hand, who walks among the seven golden lampstands" (2:1, cf. 1:20). This is a declaration of the continuing presence of Christ with his people and his care and concern for them.

The message of each of the seven letters is directed to the angel of the particular church that is mentioned. The term *angel* in this context could denote the local church leader, or it could refer to the spiritual guardian angel of that church. Certainly the consistent usage of the word elsewhere in the book argues strongly for the latter view.

The opening words, "I know," to each of the seven churches indicates that Christ knows the special circumstances of that church. Consequently the statement that follows is either commendation for faithfulness in Christian commitment, or condemnation for slackness and unfaithfulness. Although the letters differ in length in accord with the needs of each community, all conclude with an appeal to hold fast and to listen to what the Spirit is saying to the churches. Each church is promised that everyone who conquers will be rewarded by Christ. The word *conquer* is a military term. It suggests that the Christian life, so far from being a bed of roses, involves a struggle against anyone and anything that saps the Christian life of all that gives it strength and power.

THE LETTER TO THE CHURCH IN EPHESUS
(REVELATION 2:1-7)

Ephesus was the principal city of Asia Minor, with a population of about 250,000. It was wealthy and cosmopolitan. Trade passed through it by land and water; it bustled with commercial life. Ephesus could also boast of having one of the seven wonders of the ancient world: the temple of Diana (or Artemis, as she was called by the Greeks), the great mother goddess. Ancient descriptions of the temple, as well as its depiction on ancient coins, testify to the architectural grandeur of the building. Standing on a platform measuring more than one hundred thousand square feet (twice the size of an American football field), the temple itself consisted of one hundred columns. Each was a monolith of marble fifty-five feet in height, and the eighteen at each end were sculptured. The internal ornamentation was of extraordinary splendor, adorned by works of art created by famous Greek artists. From all parts of the Mediterranean world tourists and devotees came to view and to worship in the great temple.

The Christian faith was established at Ephesus in the 60s of the first century. Paul had spent three years there during his third missionary journey (Acts 20:31). One result of his preaching was the reduction in the sale of silver souvenirs of the temple of Diana. The book of Acts (19:21-41) tells of the uproar that occurred when the guild of silversmiths, fearful that their sales would keep falling away, started a riot in order to prevent further Christian influence from hurting their business.

On a subsequent visit when Paul took leave of the elders of the church at Ephesus, he warned them, with tears in his eyes, that they were in for a time of trouble. These are his words: "I know that after I have gone, savage wolves will come in among you, not sparing the flock. Some even from your own group will come distorting the truth in order to entice the disciples to follow them" (Acts 20:29-30). It is to this church at Ephesus that John is writing in the 90s when the second generation of believers makes up the congregation. What Paul had foreseen in the 60s has now occurred. False leaders have arisen and are leading believers astray. To this church the heavenly Christ says: "I know your works, your toil and your patient endurance. I know that you cannot tolerate evildoers; you have tested those who claim to be apostles but are not, and have found them to be false" (2:2).

These words are followed by words of condemnation: "But I have this against you, that you have abandoned the love you

31

had at first" (2:4). The Ephesians had made a good start. They had weeded out those who were spreading ideas that did not ring true according to the apostolic faith.[2] But the weeding-out process had been achieved at a high cost. The love for Christ they had at first had grown cold; also the love they used to have for other believers was replaced by suspicions of unsound teaching.

Anyone who has attended a church or parish meeting on some matter of principle knows how easily divisive situations arise. At Ephesus there had been the separation of those who should be together. Therefore the heavenly Christ warns the readers: "Repent, and do the works you did at first. If not, I will come to you and remove your lampstand from its place, unless you repent" (2:5). The presence of Christ departs when well-intentioned people, zealous to find the right way, depart from the ultimate way, which is love.

The letter concludes with an exhortation and a promise: "Let anyone who has an ear listen to what the Spirit is saying to the churches" (2:7). Of course everyone has ears, but the sense here is that everyone who has spiritual perception should listen. The promise is, " To everyone who conquers, I will give permission to eat from the tree of life that is the paradise of God" (2:7). The tree of life, which had been denied to Adam (Gen. 3:22), is now accessible to the conqueror; to the person, that is, who obeys the message of the letter and overcomes in the conflict with evil.

THE LETTER TO THE CHURCH IN SMYRNA
(REVELATION 2:8-11)

The messenger, traveling about thirty-five miles north from Ephesus, would reach another of the great cities of Asia Minor—Smyrna (Izmir, on today's map). A city of great antiq-

---

2. On the "works of the Nicolaitans" (2:6), see the comments on 2:14-15 (p. 35 below).

uity, Smyrna became a large and prosperous commercial center. The city was renowned for its loyalty to Rome and its ritual worship of the emperor. Almost three hundred years before the writing of Revelation the first temple in the world dedicated to the goddess Roma was built in Smyrna. Seventy years before John's banishment the city dedicated a magnificent temple in honor of the Emperor Tiberius. Thereafter it was a center of worship of both Rome and Caesar.

The letter to the church in Smyrna is the shortest of the seven messages and, like the letter to the church in Philadelphia, contains no condemnation, only commendation. The Christians at Smyrna had to endure persecution and deprivation, due no doubt to their refusal to take part in ceremonies connected with emperor worship. In addition to poverty, the Christians of Smyrna had to bear with the lies spread by certain Jews, who were accusing them of being agitators against the civil authorities (2:9).

Christ's exhortation to these persecuted believers was to be faithful to the extent of being ready to die for his sake (2:10). Opposition to the gospel was so fierce that martyrdom appeared to be a real possibility. Indeed, one of the best-known Christian martyrs of all ages was a native of Smyrna. This was Polycarp, who, according to both Irenaeus and Tertullian, had been consecrated bishop of Smyrna by John himself. Undoubtedly, he would have read this letter and pondered its message. Perhaps it was a source of strength to him when his hour of martyrdom came in February of the year 156.

To the faithful at Smyrna who do not flinch, Christ promises to give "the crown of life" (2:10). In Greek there are two words that can be translated "crown." One is *diadēma,* which means a royal crown; the other, which is used here, is *stephanos,* which usually has something to do with joy and victory. John is referring to the garlands that were presented to the winners at the Olympic and other games.

To the faithful another promise is made: they " will not be harmed by the second death." What is the second death? Our first death happens when we take our last breath on earth. The second death comes to impenitent sinners at the Final Judgment. Later in the book (see p. 96) John is more specific about what this involves, and who will suffer it (20:6, 14; 21:8; cf. also the words of Jesus in Matt. 10:28 and Luke 12:4-5).

THE LETTER TO THE CHURCH IN PERGAMUM
(REVELATION 2:12-17)

Pergamum, about fifty miles north of Smyrna, was a city that had many claims to distinction. Since the second century before Christ it was the capital of the Roman province of Asia. The city was renowned for its library, which rivaled the famous library at Alexandria and has left a monument to that name in our word *parchment* (derived from "Pergamum"). No traveler could visit Pergamum without being impressed by its welter of temples and altars. Temples to innumerable pagan gods dotted the city. Behind the city was a terraced hill on which stood an immense altar to Zeus. The altar stood on a huge platform surrounded by colonnades, and the whole structure looked like an enormous throne. On this platform animal sacrifices were burned twenty-four hours a day by a constantly changing team of priests. The overpowering smell of burning animal flesh permeated the air in Pergamum, and all day long a column of smoke could be seen from miles around, serving to keep the supremacy of Zeus ever in the public eye.

Pergamum was also a center for the worship of Asclepius, the god of healing. Sanatoria were attached to the temples where the sick were laid in the hope that one of the sacred snakes would touch and heal them. (The serpent was Asclepius's symbol, and it is still depicted in the caduceus, the insignia of medical associations.) To John, however, the serpent was a symbol of the personification of evil, "that ancient serpent, who is called the Devil and Satan" (12:9). In view of such a multiplicity of forms of paganism, it is not surprising that the heavenly Christ writes to the church in Pergamum, "I know where you are living, where Satan's throne is" (2:13).

Pergamum was not an easy city for Christians to live in, and it must have been a great comfort for believers there to know that the Lord knew what they were experiencing. Hostility to the church was determined and more vicious in Pergamum than in many other towns. There had been real persecution, and a believer named Antipas had been put to death (2:13) in order to persuade the others to forsake their faith, and to discourage others from becoming Christians.

The church, however, needed help not only against enemies outside but also against enemies within. Some members held "to the teaching of the Nicolaitans" (2:15). The sect against whose works the church at Ephesus had been warned (2:6) had also made inroads at Pergamum. According to Acts 15:29, the Jerusalem church had earlier advised Gentile converts to abstain from food sacrificed to idols. However, Christians interpreted this advice in different ways. Paul clearly regarded it as meaning that believers should not take part in sacrificial meals held at pagan shrines, but were otherwise free to eat whatever was put in front of them, and to buy whatever was sold in the market (1 Cor. 8:7-13; 10:20-21). Most of the meat sold in the market came from temples, where it had been sacrificed to a god—but only a token part was burnt on the altar, and the rest was sold. We do not know what sort of rules the churches in Asia followed. But it seems clear from the sternness of this message to Pergamum that Christians there had adopted a life-style very similar to that of their environment. In fact, their adaptation to the non-Christian environment also involved an equally permissive attitude to the lax sexual morality of the Nicolaitans (2:14-15). The Lord tells them to repent, otherwise they will be punished (2:16).

To those who stand firm against both persecution and false teachings the Lord promises to give some of the hidden manna (2:17). Manna was the food supplied by God to the

Israelites during their long journey from Egypt to the promised land (Exod. 16:32-34). Besides the hidden manna, the heavenly Christ promises to "give a white stone, and on the white stone is written a new name that no one knows except the one who receives it" (2:17). In ancient times a white stone was greatly prized, either as an amulet, especially if the name of some deity was engraved upon it, or as a mark of membership in a special group.

THE LETTER TO THE CHURCH IN THYATIRA
(REVELATION 2:18-29)

Thyatira, about forty-five miles southeast on the road from Pergamum to Sardis, was a town of considerable commercial importance in which there were many traders and artisans. Ancient records indicate the presence there of many trade guilds. Archaeologists have found inscriptions that mention guilds of woolworkers, linen workers, makers of outer garments, dyers, leatherworkers, tanners, potters, bakers, slave dealers, and bronzesmiths. Such guilds combined some of the features of our modern trade unions with certain religious features. Banquets of the members of the guild often took place within a pagan temple or shrine, where an animal was offered to the gods and then eaten by the members of the guild.

This obviously put Christians in a difficult dilemma. If they did not participate in such feasts and ceremonies of the guild, they would be unable to make a living. If they did participate, they were being unfaithful to the Lord.

Christ begins the letter to Thyatira by commending the devout Christians there for their efforts to remain faithful: "I know your works—your love, faith, service, and patient endurance" (2:19). It is good to read, "I know that your last works are greater than the first." There is progress in the life of this congregation, which forms a contrast to the church in Ephesus where the members are reprimanded for having fallen back (2:4). There is much to commend at Thyatira.

At the same time, the church at Thyatira was guilty of tolerating a woman "who calls herself a prophet" (2:20). John identifies her with the name of her Old Testament counterpart, Jezebel, Ahab's Phoenician queen, who corrupted the faith of Israel with "the many whoredoms and sorceries" of her native gods, Baal and Astarte (2 Kings 9:22; cf. 1 Kings 16:31-33). The heavenly Christ had called the would-be prophet to repentance, but she refused "to repent of her fornication" (2:21). Here the word *fornication* is probably used in the Old Testament sense of apostasy. Her teaching of what the writer witheringly calls "the deep things of Satan" (2:24) had the effect of compromising Christian commitment by taking part in pagan practices. We should not minimize the importance of problems confronting first-century Christians, for it was economic suicide to reject the minimum requirements for guild membership. Nor should we dismiss this problem as only of academic interest, as if it does not concern us. Every generation of Christians must face the question: How far should I accept and adopt contemporary standards and practices?

To the usual phrase, "everyone who conquers," there is added "and continues to do my works to the end" (2:26)— where "my works" is contrasted with "her doings." "To the end" suggests that perseverance in the Christian life is all-important.

Two rewards are promised to those who conquer: they will share in Christ's messianic rule over the nations (2:26), and to them Christ will give the morning star (2:28). The promise of the gift of the morning star is, of course, not to be understood literalistically as the bestowal of millions of tons of inert matter; the expression is a metaphor announcing the dawn of a new day and the fulfillment of hope after the night of longing and expectation. In fact, John's symbolism of "morning star" is indicated at the very end of his book where the Lord describes himself as "the bright morning star" (22:16). In pledging to give this star to the conqueror, Christ is pledging to give himself. The ultimate reward enjoyed by Christians is to be with their Lord.

4

MORE LETTERS TO CHURCHES

(Revelation 3:1-22)

THE LETTER TO THE CHURCH IN SARDIS
(REVELATION 3:1-6)

S ARDIS, a busy commercial and industrial city at the junction of five roads about thirty miles south of Thyatira, had been the capital of the ancient region called Lydia. In the sixth century B.C. it was one of the greatest cities of the world, where the fabulous King Croesus reigned amid his treasures. Even though the citadel of Sardis was situated on an almost impregnable hill with sheer cliffs on three sides that dropped some fifteen hundred feet to the valley below, the city had twice suffered humiliating defeats. In the sixth century B.C., because of lack of vigilance, the city experienced a stealthy attack by the Persians, and once again, through the negligence of its defenders, Sardis was captured by Antiochus the Great in 214 B.C. Still later in its history, in A.D. 17 the city was devastated by a catastrophic earthquake. Through the generosity of the Emperor Tiberius, who remitted the taxes for five years, the city was rebuilt, and began once again to flourish as a woolen center. Although the city had lost most of its former glory, it was still known for its wealth, and also for its luxurious and licentious living.

To the church in Sardis, Christ presents himself as the one who has "the seven spirits of God and the seven stars" (3:1). These words indicate his sovereign control over churches and the source of spiritual power. Certainly the church at Sardis needed just such a reminder, for this congregation, though having a "name of being alive," was in fact "dead" (3:1). No condemnation could be sharper; the church was an example of merely nominal Christianity.

And yet the Lord does not begin the letter with threats; he begins with a series of urgent admonitions: "Wake up, and strengthen what remains. . . . Remember then what you received and heard; obey it, and repent" (3:2-3). Here are five staccato imperatives: Wake up! Strengthen what remains! Remember! Obey! Repent!

As the city had fallen in the past because of lack of vigilance, so now the Sardians are reminded to be watchful and to shake off their apathy. If, however, they "do not wake up," Christ says, "I will come like a thief "—that is to say, he will come at an unexpected hour. This is not a reference to the Second Coming, which will take place whether the Sardians are watchful or not. Christ comes in many ways and at many times, and this is clearly a limited coming in judgment upon the unrepentant.

The situation at Sardis was critical but not hopeless. There were "still a few persons in Sardis who had not soiled their clothes" (3:4). Archaeologists have found inscriptions posted in pagan shrines in Asia Minor that indicate that those who wore dirty clothing were excluded from worship because they were an insult to the gods. But the meaning here is probably symbolic, with clothes symbolizing the purity of their Christian life (see Zech. 3:3-5).

Christ's promise to the faithful few is that henceforth "they will walk with me, dressed in white, for they are worthy" (3:4). Members of the Jewish sect of the Essenes at Qumran wore white garments as a symbol of their inner purity. White was the color used by the Roman emperor in a triumphal procession. In the Old Testament white garments signify heaven (Dan. 7:9) and festivity (Eccles. 9:8). All these symbols are included here with the emphasis on victory: "If you conquer, you will be clothed like them in white robes" (3:5).

A further promise made by Christ to faithful Christians is phrased negatively: "I will not blot your name out of the book of life" (3:5). In ancient cities the names of citizens were kept in registers and were erased upon death or the commission of a treasonous act. The idea of writing names in the book of life had a long history in Judaism. Moses prayed that if God would not forgive the sin of the Israelites in the golden calf episode, he wished to be blotted out "of the book that you have written" (Exod. 32:32; cf. Ps. 69:28). By the time of Daniel the theme had developed to include the idea of books being opened on the day of judgment (Dan. 7:10; 12:1). The idea of a divine register is found frequently in the New Testament; it is referred to by Jesus (Luke 10:20), Paul (Phil. 4:3), and especially John, who often refers to such records (Rev. 3:5; 13:8; 17:8; 20:12, 15; 21:27), but says nothing about the manner in which they are kept.

The final promise is directed to those who conquer, "I will confess your name before my Father and before his angels" (3:5), and is a repetition of Jesus' pronouncement in the Gospels that he would acknowledge those who acknowledge him before others (Matt. 10:32; Luke 12:8). The concluding words of the letter are thus a challenge to the readers to be faithful.

THE LETTER TO THE CHURCH IN PHILADELPHIA
(REVELATION 3:7-13)

Philadelphia was about thirty-five miles southeast of Sardis. The city had been founded in the second century B.C. by Attalus II Philadelphos, one of the kings of Pergamum, and was the youngest of the seven cities. *Philadelphos* is the Greek word that means "one who loves his brother." Such was the affection of Attalus for his brother Eumenes that he was called Philadelphos, and it was after him that Philadelphia was named.

The ancient historian Strabo called Philadelphia "a city full of earthquakes." Earth tremors were frequent, and had caused many former inhabitants to leave the city for a safer home in the surrounding country. The severe earthquake of A.D. 17, which had devastated Sardis, almost completely demolished Philadelphia. But by the 90s, with the aid of an imperial subsidy, Philadelphia had been rebuilt, and within the city there was a congregation of Christian believers.

The church in Philadelphia was very different from the church in Sardis. It was poor, small, and harassed both by pagan citizens and by the local synagogue; but its members had not strayed from the way. The letter to Sardis contains almost unmitigated censure; the letter to Philadelphia is one of almost unqualified commendation. The opening formula, "I know your works," is followed by no word of reproof but by the declaration, "I have set before you an open door" (3:8). What is this door that has been opened wide and that "no one is able to shut"? In Christian understanding, a "door" was a technical expression for an opportunity for spreading the gospel (see 1 Cor. 16:9; 2 Cor. 2:12; Col. 4:3). The church, though small, had a great missionary task to perform.

The missionary zeal of the church, however, had been met with opposition. The source of this opposition appeared to have come from the Jewish population of the city, who rejected the claim of Christians to be the spiritual Israel. Since John himself had been born a Jew, we must not take the expression "those of the synagogue of Satan" (3:9) in an anti-Jewish or anti-Semitic sense. The synagogue at Philadelphia was criticized, not for being Jewish, but for being hostile to Christians. The authorities of the synagogue would undoubtedly have excommunicated any of their group who confessed Jesus as the Messiah. Never mind, says Christ; the time will come when those who have resisted the gospel will yet recognize the church as the true "Israel of God" (see Gal. 6:16) and "will learn that I have loved you" (3:9).

A reward is promised to this little church. Because it had faithfully kept "my word of patient endurance," Christ says, "I will keep you from the hour of trial that is coming on the whole world to test the inhabitants of the earth" (3:10). The phrase "the inhabitants of the earth" is an expression used elsewhere in Revelation to refer to the enemies of the church. This is the first indication in the book of an approaching general visitation, which will be portrayed in the successive series of judgment-visions from chapter 6 onward. It is not easy to determine whether the promise, "I will keep you from the hour of trial" (3:10), means "keep you from undergoing the trial" or "keep you throughout the trial." But the promise can scarcely mean entire escape from suffering, because the promise to the one who conquers (verse 12) shows that there will be martyrs. It appears, therefore, that the Philadelphia church will not be spared from testing. It will be kept *in*, not *from*, the time of trouble.

The special reward promised to the one who conquers is addressed (as in each of the seven letters) to the individual members of the church: "I will make you a pillar in the temple of my God; you will never go out of it" (3:12). The idea of making the victor a pillar in God's temple is clearly symbolic, for later in the book John will insist that there is no need for a temple in God's city (21:22). John is not in the slightest concerned to keep the details of one vision consistent with those of another. In each he is making a point with emphasis, and we should not try to dovetail one vision into the details of another. Apocalyptic imagery is sufficiently fluid to allow the figure of a temple in one vision and to dismiss it in another.

The metaphor of a pillar in God's temple can be understood either as a pillar supporting the roof of the sanctuary, or as a freestanding pillar as a lasting monument. Then as now it was customary to erect such pillars or columns with inscriptions to celebrate the lives or victories of great leaders. In any case, the point seems to be that the pillar will not be moved from its base, as had happened to many pillars in earthquake-prone Philadelphia.

The letter closes with the same exhortation that appears at the end of each letter, "Let anyone who has an ear listen to what the Spirit is saying to the churches" (3:13). The message to each church is at the same time a message to all churches.

THE LETTER TO THE CHURCH IN LAODICEA
(REVELATION 3:14-22)

Laodicea completed the semicircle of cities to which, starting at Ephesus, a person would have traveled in order to deliver the seven messages. It was about one hundred miles east of Ephesus and about forty miles southeast of Philadelphia. The city was founded about the middle of the third century B.C. by Antiochus II of Syria and named in honor of his wife Laodice.

Laodicea was one of the richest commercial centers of Asia Minor. A severe earthquake devastated the city in A.D. 61, but so rich and independent were its citizens that they refused financial assistance from the Roman government, and out of their own resources and by their own efforts they eventually rebuilt their city. Laodicea was noted for its textile products; the local wool, said to be even softer than that of Miletus, was raven-black in color. The city was also the chief medical center of Phrygia, and was famous for its eye salve, which was exported far and wide.

Laodicea, Hierapolis, and Colossae formed a cluster of cities that were evangelized in the 60s during Paul's Ephesian ministry (Acts 19:10)—not by Paul in person but, as it appears, by his colleague, Epaphras (Col. 4:12-13). Paul, however, regarded those cities as part of his appointed mission field (Col. 2:1), and asked the Colossian Christians to convey his greetings to believers in Laodicea—among whom "Nympha and the church in her house" are specially mentioned (Col. 4:15).

By the 90s of the first century the spiritual condition of the church in Laodicea had deteriorated sadly. The decline of the church may have been due in part to the material wealth of its members and to the luxury of their life-style. In any case, this church receives the severest condemnation of the seven to which John is bidden to write.

As in the other letters, the heavenly Christ is introduced by a brief description that accents his mysterious divine-human personality. To the Laodiceans he writes as "the Amen" (3:14). This Hebrew word is familiar to us through its use at the end of prayers. But its meaning here, somewhat different from the liturgical use, is brought out by the words that immediately follow, "the faithful and true witness" (3:14). The title may have been suggested by Isaiah 65:16, where "God of faithfulness" would be literally translated "God of Amen." Jesus Christ is the perfect Amen of God, whose words and promises are true beyond all doubt. Christ is further identified as "the origin of God's creation" (3:14). He is not part of the creation, but is the moving cause behind all creation (see John 1:3; 1 Cor. 8:6; Col. 1:15, 18).

The solemnity of such titles enhances the sternness of Christ's reproof of the Laodicean church. The reprimand is the most severe in the seven letters, with no word of commendation. The church is accused (3:15-16) of being neither hot nor cold, but of being lukewarm.[1] That is, among its membership were those who thought there might be a middle ground between worshiping God and worshiping the emperor; that in some way they could remain in the Christian church while at the same time obeying the emperor's command to worship

---

1. The Laodicean church is the only one of the seven to add an adjective to the English language—and a pretty discreditable one at that! The word *Laodicean* is defined in the *American Heritage Dictionary* as "indifferent or lukewarm esp. in religion."

him. On the contrary, in their loyalty to Christ they must be "hot"; those who were content to be "lukewarm" might just as well go to the extreme of being completely "cold." Tepid religion is nauseating, and the Lord of the church expresses in the strongest way his repudiation of the church by the warning, "I am about to spit you out of my mouth" (3:16). Their boast of material sufficiency ("You say, 'I am rich, I have prospered, and I need nothing'") is deceptive, and shows a proud, smug self-complacency. Materially affluent and self-satisfied, the church is spiritually "wretched, pitiable, poor, blind, and naked" (3:17). There is some irony in these words, which contrast sharply with the achievements at Laodicea in banking, medicine, and the manufacture of clothing.

To such a church Christ gives his solemn admonition, "I counsel you to buy from me gold refined by fire" (3:18). The parallel with Isaiah 55:1, "You that have no money, . . . come, buy wine and milk without money and without price," shows that "buying" is figurative for obtaining. Christ admonishes the church to realize that it is actually poor in spirituality and that it needs to obtain from him the gifts that cannot be purchased with money.

Somewhat abruptly, the author changes from his rather harsh denunciation to an approach of affection and tender concern. The proper response to divine correction is to "be earnest, therefore, and repent" (3:19). This is the fifth call to repentance in these letters (see 2:5, 16, 21; 3:3); Smyrna and Philadelphia alone needed no such admonition. Laodicea's repentance would involve the replacement of complacency with zealous concern.

To the call to repentance Christ adds the most tender message found in any of the seven letters. "Listen! I am standing at the door, knocking; if you hear my voice and open the door, I will come in to you and eat with you, and you with me" (3:20). Christ's knocking on the door is a simple but profound picture of grace and free will in action. The scene

45

has been unforgettably captured by Holman Hunt in his famous painting, *The Light of the World*. The Lord has come and is knocking at the door, but there is no handle or latch on the outside of the door; it must be opened from within. Christ promises to enter when the resident opens the door. More than that, the image of eating with the Lord symbolizes the joy of fellowship. In the Near East the sharing of a common meal indicates the forming of a strong bond of affection and companionship. As such it became a common symbol of the intimacy to be enjoyed in the coming messianic kingdom.

The concluding promise belongs to the coming age and is limited to those who conquer, that is, to those who win in the struggle against self-indulgence, self-confidence, and self-satisfaction. To all such Christ promises, "I will give [you] a place with me on my throne, just as I myself conquered and sat down with my Father on his throne" (3:21). The promise to rule with Christ is one that is made often (1:6; 5:10; 20:6; 22:5; see also Matt. 19:28; Luke 22:28-30; 2 Tim. 2:12). The symbolism of the throne signifies royal honor—and a place with Christ is the highest honor conceivable for a Christian.

In the final verse we hear for the seventh and last time the exhortation, "Listen to what the Spirit is saying to the churches" (3:22). It is noteworthy that although each letter is addressed to a different church, the concluding formula refers to "the churches." That is, the message to each church is at the same time a message to all churches. The seven churches provide examples of the kinds of things that can go wrong in any church. These are the danger of losing the love that one had at first (Ephesus), fear of suffering (Smyrna), doctrinal compromise (Pergamum), moral compromise (Thyatira), spiritual deadness (Sardis), failure to hold fast (Philadelphia), and lukewarmness (Laodicea).

5

JOHN'S VISION
OF GOD AND THE LAMB

(Revelation 4:1–5:14)

U NLIKE chapters 2 and 3, which are focused on the conditions of seven churches located in western Asia Minor, the focus of chapters 4 and 5 is heaven. They describe John's vision of God on the throne and of the Lamb of God, who is of course Jesus Christ. Until now the symbols in Revelation have been relatively straightforward and their meaning relatively easy to understand. From here onward they become more difficult and complex. Nevertheless, by using a disciplined imagination one can follow the author's meaning, at least to some degree.

John begins by saying that he saw a door standing open in heaven and heard a trumpet-like voice saying, "Come up here, and I will show you what must take place after this" (4:1). In the Greek language in which the book was written the word translated "open" signifies not only that the door to heaven stood open but that it remains open. Thus the way is clear for others as well as the seer to appreciate the splendor and majesty of the heavenly scene.

On hearing the trumpet-like voice John at once sensed that he "was in the spirit," an awareness continuing or corresponding to his experience referred to in 1:10, "I was in the spirit on the Lord's day." This now enabled him to respond to the invitation, "Come up here," and to describe what he saw and heard after passing through the door opened in heaven. There he gazed on the majestic spectacle of a throne and of the Lord God Almighty seated on the throne (4:2). Here the New Revised Standard Version punctuates the sentence with an exclamation mark in order to suggest something of the profound awe that John experienced during his vision. In what follows he attempts to describe the transcendental glory and grandeur of God who reigns from the throne. But how was he to convey the dazzling brilliance of this exalted scene? The finite languages of earth are incapable of defining the infinite realities that John saw in heaven; hence he must use earthly analogies, but always with the understanding that the heavenly reality far surpasses the earthly symbol.

In accord with the reluctance of Jewish writers to picture God, John carefully avoids any descriptive detail. No form is visible, and the writer refrains from even mentioning the august name of God. He says that the one seated on the throne "looks like jasper and carnelian" (4:3). These are two precious or semiprecious stones. There are several kinds of what in ancient times was called jasper; probably John has in mind a translucent type of jasper, which is clear as crystal (see also 21:11). When such a stone is polished it sparkles and flashes with luminous splendor. Is not this a beautiful and poetic way to draw attention to what other biblical writers refer to as the holiness and glory of God?

In addition to jasper, John tells us that God looks like carnelian. This gemstone is usually a deep reddish color. When one holds a carnelian in one's hand, it seems as though a fire is smoldering inside the stone. Does John mean to suggest that, in addition to the holiness of God, God also burns in wrath against sin? If this is what is suggested, then John's conception of God is altogether like that of other biblical authors.

Continuing to contemplate the vision of God seated upon

the throne, John notices that "around the throne is a rainbow that looks like an emerald" (4:3). For the Jews the rainbow was the sign of the covenant of God's mercy. According to the book of Genesis, after the flood God declared to Noah that though humankind might again fall into grievous sin, "never again shall there be a flood to destroy the earth." As a pledge of mercy God declared, "I have set my bow in the clouds, and it shall be a sign of the covenant" (Gen. 9:11, 13). So when John says that he saw a rainbow arching over and around the throne of God, he is suggesting that God is merciful in all that he does. John of course knew that a rainbow has a whole spectrum of colors, but he says that this rainbow is emerald green in color. Green is soothing, like meadows and distant forests. Could this mean that after having been exposed to the brilliance of God's holiness and the heat of God's wrath against sin, the man of Patmos is comforted by the assurance of divine mercy that overarches all of God's deeds?

If we are correct in understanding the import of John's words, then we can appreciate that his concept of the nature of God is altogether in keeping with the theology taught elsewhere in the Scriptures. The difference involves only the manner in which John expresses himself, namely by means of evocative poetic symbolism. Such descriptions would come as a tonic to persecuted Christians, reminding them of the splendor and majesty and power of God that are projected by these scintillating images of the divine Presence and the radiance surrounding the throne.

We must acknowledge, however, that other parts of the description of John's vision are less clear to us. The precise meaning of some of the details is anybody's guess. Who are the "twenty-four elders, dressed in white robes, with golden crowns on their heads" (4:4)? Seated on thrones around the throne of God, these elders may represent the twelve patriarchs of the Old Testament and the twelve apostles of the New Testament, symbolizing the two covenants of the people of God. Their thrones and white garments suggest that they are kingly priests, while their crowns represent the idea of reigning. The awesome vision is enhanced by "flashes of lightning, and rumblings and peals of thunder" that issue from the throne (4:5). One is reminded of similar visible and audible manifestations of God's presence on Sinai prior to giving the law to Moses (Exod. 19:16). In Hebrew poetry the thunderstorm suggests God's presence and majesty (1 Sam. 2:10).

Between John and the throne is a flat pavement-like surface, "like a sea of glass, like crystal" (4:6). The God of Israel had once seemed to stand on "something like a pavement of sapphire stone" (Exod. 24:10). John is probably alluding to this passage in Exodus and wishes to stress the magnificence of the throne and the distance still remaining between him and the throne. The description here could well have been linked to the expanse of the Aegean Sea viewed on a still, clear day from the hills of Patmos. The picture is one of immense distance and serenity.

John's description of the four living creatures on each side of the throne has a literary background that derives from the first chapter of the book of Ezekiel. They represent the cherubim, though John also supplies some of the features of the seraphim from Isaiah's vision of God in the temple (Isa. 6:2). The cherubim were not at all like chubby infants advertising baby soap, but they appear to be God's strong agents, representing power over all the created world. The four creatures in John's vision (4:7) have the appearance of a lion, an ox, a human being, and a flying eagle. These symbolize, respectively, what is the noblest, strongest, wisest, and swiftest in creation. In subsequent centuries it was customary to associate these four figures with the four evangelists, generally the man with Matthew, the lion with Mark, the ox with Luke, and the eagle with John. Such association, which is entirely fanciful, has influenced many forms of Christian art.

The four living creatures, John says, are "full of eyes in front and behind" (4:6), and each has six wings, "full of eyes all around and inside" (4:8). The repeated phrase "full of eyes" suggests unsleeping watchfulness, as the creatures perceive everything in every direction. One should not attempt to picture these creatures literally; no diagram can show all these characteristics.

The function of the four living creatures, who are mentioned fourteen times in the book, is to act, so to say, as choirmasters leading all the public worship in heaven constantly praising God, enthroned in majesty. "Whenever the living creatures give glory and honor and thanks" to the eternal one (4:9), the twenty-four elders prostrate themselves before the throne. In typical oriental fashion they lay down their crowns as a sign of their homage, and as a dramatic demonstration of their acknowledgment of God's sovereignty. The crowns are God's gifts and are appropriately given back to God in worship.

The ceaseless worship of the four living creatures (4:8) does not imply that this worship is their sole activity, but rather that it is their constant disposition—their every action is an expression of adoration.

Joined by the twenty-four elders, the four living creatures give voice to two songs, probably examples of early congregational praise. One of the hymns, beginning "Holy, holy, holy" (4:8), celebrates the otherness of God, that is, the distinction between the Infinite and all finite beings. As in Isaiah's vision of "the Lord sitting on a throne, high and lofty" (Isa. 6:1-3), the threefold repetition of "holy" designates the superlative degree. God alone is the holiest, most powerful and everlasting one. The second hymn praises God as creator: "You are worthy, our Lord and God, to receive glory and honor and power, for you created all things, and by your will they existed and were created" (4:11). Here the twenty-four elders ascribe to the Creator the name that the Emperor Domitian had usurped, "our Lord and God" (see p. 16 above). Only God is worthy to receive the glory and the honor and the power, where the use of the definite article with each of the three nouns in the Greek indicates totality.

The account of John's vision continues in chapter 5, when John's attention is drawn to a scroll that is held in the right hand of the one seated upon the throne. Written on the inside and on the back, it was sealed with seven seals (5:1). The scroll is the book of the eternal decrees of God. The fact that there are seven seals indicates that its contents are completely hidden, so that "no one in heaven or on earth or under the earth was able to open the scroll or to look into it" (5:3).

John began to weep bitterly because no one could be found who was worthy to open the scroll or able to carry out God's plan for human history. Then one of the elders said, "Do not weep. See, the Lion of the tribe of Judah, the Root of David, has conquered, so that he can open the scroll and its seven seals" (5:5).

What follows is altogether unexpected. John looked to see the Lion, the king of beasts, and instead he sees a Lamb with the marks of slaughter upon it (5:6)! He looked to see power and force, by which the enemies of his faith would be destroyed, and he sees sacrificial love and gentleness as the way to win the victory. The might of Christ is the power of love. Most Jews had been expecting a Messiah who would break the yoke of the Roman imperial power and liberate his people. The expressions "Lion of the tribe of Judah" and "Root of David" were recognized as scriptural references (Gen. 49:9; Isa. 11:1, 10) pointing to the coming Messiah.

The fundamental transformation of the messianic expectation became obvious on that first Palm Sunday when Jesus presented himself as God's Messiah. He rode into Jerusalem, not on a war horse, equipped with all kinds of armor, but on a donkey, a symbol of peace and humility. Instead of a ferocious lion that hurts others, the Messiah is a sacrificial lamb that takes into himself the hurts of others. According to Isaiah 53:5, which has colored the Christian understanding of the mission of Jesus, "He was wounded for our transgressions, crushed for our iniquities; . . . and by his bruises we are healed."

Perhaps we can appreciate something of the quite staggering effect of this transformation of images. Here the Lamb, who alone in all the universe is able to understand the hidden decrees of God, and who alone is able to put them into effect, came and "took the scroll from the right hand of the one who was seated on the throne" (5:7). One should not ask how a four-hoofed creature can take a scroll and open its seals! The poetic symbolism of the author is heightened still further when the Lamb is described as having seven horns and seven eyes. This should not be taken as a literal description. Rather, the seven horns mean that Christ has complete power, and the seven eyes mean that he sees and knows all things. Compare the repeated "I know . . ." at the opening of each of the seven letters of the churches in chapters 2 and 3, as well as the penetrating gaze of him whose eyes are like a flame of fire (1:14; 2:18; 19:12). In opening the scroll, the Lamb is about to disclose what the scroll contains. In short, Jesus does not change the divine plan; he unfolds its eternal and unchangeable nature by his obedience, even unto death on the cross.

No wonder there is praise in heaven, accompanied by incense and harps. The twenty-four elders fall before the Lamb and offer "golden bowls full of incense, which are the prayers of the saints" (5:8). Here is John's first hint of the participation of the church's worship on earth with that of the church in heaven. This idea appears also near the close of the Apostles' Creed, when Christians confess that they believe "in the communion of saints." This communion of saints is not just the fellowship we enjoy with other people during a service of worship, but it includes also the idea that John expresses here—the unity of worship of the church militant on earth with that of the church triumphant in heaven. The prayers of believers here on earth are mingled with the worship of angels and archangels and all the host of heaven, in adoration of God and the Lamb.

In words that recollect the praise offered to God for having created all things (4:11), so now a new song is sung in praise of the Lamb: "You are worthy to take the scroll and to open its seals, for you were slaughtered and by your blood you ransomed for God saints from every tribe and language and people and nation" (5:9). Here there is a hint that just as the Passover lamb's blood protected the firstborn of the Israelites from the plague of death, so too "the Lamb of God who takes away the sin of the world" (John 1:29) will protect the faithful from the wrath to come. Suddenly the power of the scene and the song is picked up by an innumerable host of angels, numbering "myriads of myriads and thousands of thousands" (5:11). Mathematically this works out to one hundred million plus one million, but probably John simply means an infinite number. The angels repeat three of the elders' terms of praise: glory, honor, and power, and add wealth, wisdom, might, and blessing (5:13). The seven terms symbolize the fullness of the praise.

Then, with thrilling crescendo, the climax and grand finale are reached. Not only do the four living creatures, the elders, and the angels unite, but all creation joins in adoration and praise to God and to the Lamb. The chapter concludes with a great "Amen!" as the elders fall down in worship.

And so, with these glorious affirmations of the goodness and mercy of God Almighty and of the Lamb ringing in John's ears, he can endure with confidence, despite the terrors about to be let loose on the world described in the following chapters. The author's primary purpose is not so much to describe the liturgy of heaven, as to give hope and a sense of victory to his people on earth in the struggle that lies ahead.

6

OPENING THE SEVEN SEALS OF GOD'S SCROLL

(Revelation 6:1–8:2)

WITH the sixth chapter, the main action of the book may be said properly to begin. The section extending from chapter 6 to the end of chapter 11 is intended to bring before the reader not only the struggle of the church amid conflict and persecution, but also the judgments of God upon the church's enemies.

We should note the outline that John follows through these six chapters. The section is dramatically arranged in a series of seven scenes that are revealed as the Lamb opens each of the seven seals. The first four seals will be opened at once, and will together make up one picture. Then the fifth and sixth seals will be opened, together making up one picture. Some intermediate material leads finally to the opening of the seventh seal. The seventh seal, in turn, is really the introduction to a new series of visions. These are announced by the blowing of seven trumpets in turn. The trumpets more or less repeat the revelation of the seven seals, though they present it more from God's standpoint. Again the same outline is followed. First, four trumpets will be sounded, making one unified impression. Then the fifth and sixth trumpets, together giving one impression. After this, another series of intermediate visions, leading finally to the last of the trumpets.

Following this complicated and repetitive pattern, John preserves unity in his work, interlocking the various parts together and at the same time developing his themes. The development, however, is not in a strictly logical fashion, such as we are familiar with in Western writing; it is, rather, a product of the Semitic mind, which runs through the whole picture again and again. Thus, the seven seals and the seven trumpets essentially tell the same thing, each time emphasizing one or another aspect of the whole.

The first four seals (6:1-8) are unified by their common image, the vision of the four horsemen of the Apocalypse. The description of this vision has features borrowed from Zechariah 6:1-5, which also involves horses of various colors— red, black, white, and dappled gray. The Apocalyptist, however, borrows only the symbol of the horses and their colors, and instead of yoking the horses to chariots he sets on each of them a rider in whom the interest of the vision is centered.

The vision of the four horsemen begins when the Lamb, who has already taken the scroll from the right hand of the one seated on the throne (5:7), begins to open the seven seals one by one. The first four openings are marked by common features. Each is preceded by an utterance from one of the four living creatures, and followed by the appearance of a horse and its rider, whose significance is partly explained. But there are also many puzzling aspects. John says:

> I saw the Lamb open one of the seven seals, and I heard one of the four living creatures call out, as with a voice of thunder, "Come!" I looked, and there was a white horse! Its rider had a bow; a crown was given to him, and he came out conquering and to conquer.
>
> When he opened the second seal, I heard the second living creature call out, "Come!" And out came another horse, bright red; its rider was permitted to take peace from the earth, so that people would slaughter one another; and he was given a great sword.
>
> When he opened the third seal, I heard the third living creature call out, "Come!" I looked, and there was a black horse! Its rider held a pair of scales in his hand, and I

heard what seemed to be a voice in the midst of the four living creatures saying, "A quart of wheat for a day's pay, and three quarts of barley for a day's pay, but do not damage the olive oil and the wine!"

When he opened the fourth seal, I heard the voice of the fourth living creature call out, "Come!" I looked and there was a pale green horse! Its rider's name was Death, and Hades followed with him; they were given authority over a fourth of the earth, to kill with sword, famine, and pestilence, and by the wild animals of the earth. (6:1-8)

Notice how brief and concise this account is. Each of the four scenes is like a cameo, very small and compact. None of the four horsemen says a single word. Each rides forth in silence. We do not know in which direction they ride, because the Greek word that has been traditionally translated "Come!" may also be translated "Go!" Do they ride from heaven to earth, or from one place on earth to another place on earth? What is the significance of this vision of the four horsemen?

One of the features that distinguishes the book of Revelation from other books of the New Testament is the author's attempt to show how power fits into the divine scheme of things. John begins with the belief that all power comes from God. God is the absolute ruler of the world. But because God gave humankind free will, there is always the possibility that we might misuse the portion of power entrusted to us. When this happens, however, it does not mean that God is helpless and frustrated. The world is still God's world, and is still ruled in accordance with the eternal laws of right and wrong.

The way that God's power is manifested in the world is that the misuse of power brings on suffering and disaster. Wars, starvation, devastation—these are the means by which it is made plain that power abused is still under God's control. These are the "judgments" of God, being worked out on the plane of history.

Bearing this in mind, we can approach more sympathetically this chapter with its succession of terrible calamities. First, there is the white horse. Its rider holds a bow and he rides off on a career of conquest. The key to the meaning of this lies in the bow. It was the characteristic weapon of the mounted Parthian warriors, to whom also white was a sacred color. Parthia was a formidable neighbor on the eastern border of the Roman Empire. What is suggested here is a Parthian invasion that meets with success.

When the second seal is opened there appears a red horse. Its rider holds a huge sword, and he is "permitted to take peace from the earth, so that people would slaughter one another" (6:4). This obviously symbolizes war and bloodshed.

The third horse is black, symbolizing death, perhaps because of the darkness of the underworld. The rider holds a pair of scales in his hand, and John hears a voice saying, "A quart of wheat for a denarius, and three quarts of barley for a denarius" (6:6 RSV). A denarius was the customary wage of a laborer for one day. Usually a denarius could purchase eight to sixteen times more grain than the amounts mentioned here. In other words, warfare is followed by inflation and famine.

The fourth horseman is Death, riding a horse the color of decaying flesh. Hades, the ruler of the dead, follows close behind. We have here all the appalling aftermath of war— famine, pestilence, and the final devastation when wild animals overrun what was once the habitat of people (6:8).

Notice that these disasters are the results of the working out of God's righteous laws for the universe. God does not approve of famine and death and hell, but they are what must follow if people persist in opposing God's rule. God wills community, which is the consequence of caring and love. Ignore physical laws, like stepping off a cliff, and disaster follows. Neglect moral laws, and disaster ensues just as surely. The woes described here are the result of not taking seriously God's command to achieve community and justice. God does not will the woes, but as long as we are free agents God allows them.

So the four horsemen of the Apocalypse are brilliant little

vignettes of God's judgments working out in history. *This* is what happens in the sphere of politics whenever men and women oppose the will of God; and *this* in the military sphere; and *this* in the sphere of economics. There are few chapters in Revelation that speak more directly to our time than this part of chapter 6. In books, in newspapers, in magazine articles, and in radio broadcasts, we read and hear about the Four Horsemen of the Apocalypse, who are riding across the earth today. We hear the cry for justice; we sense that there must be a judgment in which the guilty will not be able to escape.

With the opening of the fifth and sixth seals of the scroll, the action shifts from earth to heaven (6:9-11). During a previous scene when the Lamb of God was praised by the heavenly host, the twenty-four elders were seen holding golden bowls of incense. We learned that the bowls were the prayers of the persecuted Christians for divine aid (5:8). Now as the Lamb breaks the fifth seal, the souls of these martyred Christians are under the altar in heaven, crying out for divine vengeance upon those who had shed their blood. They are told, however, that they must wait until God's appointed time; persecution must first run its course (6:11). Then all those who have suffered on Christ's account will be vindicated together. Meanwhile, the martyrs can already enjoy their rightful place in heaven; they were each given their white robe of purity, victory, and service (6:11).

With the breaking of the sixth seal by the Lamb, God's punishments of the wicked are resumed (6:12-17). In his description of these John makes use of symbolism drawn from many parts of the Old Testament: the earthquake from Haggai (2:6), the sun turned black and the moon turned to blood from Joel (2:31), the stars fallen from heaven like figs from a fig tree (Isa. 34:4), and the sky rolled up like a scroll (Isa. 34:4). The use of cosmic convulsions to describe social and political upheaval is well established in biblical prophecy (compare the picture of chaos in Jeremiah 4:23-26, where the desolation caused by foreign invaders is intended). Precisely what is denoted by the details of this highly colorful language is difficult to determine. In any case, John clearly describes the terror of an impenitent world. All classes of society, which here include the magnates of Eastern kingdoms and the generals of the Roman army, as well as "everyone, slave and free" (6:15), make a futile attempt to escape God's punishment for their oppression and persecution of the Christians. They are not so much afraid of death as of the revealed presence of God and of the righteous anger of Christ. They are heard to call to the mountains and the rocks, "Fall on us and hide us from the face of the one seated on the throne and from the wrath of the Lamb; for the great day of their wrath has come, and who is able to stand?" (6:16-17).

Between the opening of the sixth and seventh seals, there is an interlude of two consolatory visions (7:1-8 and 9-17); these provide assurance that God's people are secure from the plagues and judgments. Four angels at the four corners of the earth are seen holding back the devastating four winds of the earth, causing a temporary suspension of the plagues (7:1). This interlude of quiet is not to be understood as a time for relaxation, but as a merciful extension of the time in which the winds of judgment are restrained from harming the earth or the sea or the trees until God's elect are marked with a seal (7:2-3).

John then sees another angel flying from the east bearing "the seal of the living God" (7:2). Standing before him are 144,000, that is, 12,000 from each of the twelve tribes of Israel.[1] The twelve tribes symbolize the new Israel, the Christian church. Each individual is marked on the forehead with a seal. The idea of the king's seal would be very meaningful in the East. The signet ring worn by Eastern kings was used to

---

1. The tribe of Dan is not mentioned, perhaps because of the tradition that the Antichrist would arise from this tribe. The tradition may have had its source in Genesis 49:17 (compare the omission of the same tribe from 1 Chronicles 4–7). The total of twelve tribes is maintained by replacing the name of Joseph with the names of his two sons, Ephraim and Manasseh.

authenticate documents as official, and to mark the personal property of the king. So when the 144,000 were sealed (7:2-4), the seal was a sign that they belonged to God and were under the power and protection of God. The protection is not physical (the two witnesses in chapter 11 are killed by the beast), but spiritual. Furthermore, the explicit number, 144,000, symbolizes completeness—not one of the redeemed is missing.

In the second vision (7:9-17), John sees a great multitude that no one could count, standing before the throne and before the Lamb. They are robed in white and are carrying palm branches, denoting that they are victors. The two visions in this chapter stand in strange contrast to each other, as to location as well as in other respects. In the first vision, the throng can be counted; in the second, it is incalculably numerous. In the first, it is drawn from the twelve tribes of Israel; in the second, from every nation. In the first, it is being prepared for imminent peril; in the second, it is victorious and secure. The two visions are correlative and refer to the same people distinguished only by their location. The 144,000 on earth are about to enter a period of secular opposition. The purpose of the second vision is to bring encouragement to believers by revealing what awaits them in heaven.

One of the elders identifies the multitude clad in white as those "who have come out of the great ordeal; they have washed their robes and made them white in the blood of the Lamb" (7:14). These words, taken literally, are paradoxical; washing a garment in blood does not make it white. On the other hand, the words do convey the symbolism that is consistent throughout the New Testament. It is a vivid way of saying that their present blessedness and their fitness to appear in the presence of God have been won for them by the sacrificial death of Christ. While the benefits of redemption are provided by Christ, the redeemed also have their part to play; "they washed their robes." What John conveys to us here with startling symbolism is expressed by the apostle Paul in more prosaic language: "Work out your own salvation with fear and trembling; for it is God who is at work in you, enabling you both to will and to work for his good pleasure" (Phil. 2:12-13).

The chapter ends with words that have brought comfort and consolation to millions. There are no words more comforting in the ears of those who have been bereaved than the closing promise:

> They will hunger no more, and thirst no more; the sun will not strike them, nor any scorching heat; for the Lamb at the center of the throne will be their shepherd, and he will guide them to springs of the water of life, and God will wipe away every tear from their eyes. (7:16-17)

The sequence of the opening of the seven seals, broken by chapter 7, is now resumed: one more seal is to be opened, the last. And that, one would have thought, would be the end of the drama; after the earth had received such punishment, what more could still be in store? And so, with the seventh seal, the reader expects the final cataclysm. But nothing happens. Instead, "there was silence in heaven for about half an hour" (8:1). It is like the solemn hush before the bursting of a hurricane. The effect of the pause is to heighten the horror of the next series of God's judgments, each to be announced by the sounding of a trumpet. However, this silence in heaven may be more than merely a dramatic interlude, for John notices that the prayers of the saints are about to ascend to God (8:3-4). Is it too fanciful to suppose, as some have suggested, that everything in heaven halts so that the prayers of the saints may be heard?

7

SOUNDING THE
SEVEN TRUMPETS

(Revelation 8:3–11:19)

A FTER the prayers of the saints ascend to God (8:4), an angel fills a censer "with fire from the altar and threw it on the earth" (8:5). Then—bang! Catastrophic consequences follow. Seven angels, one after another, blow their trumpets, announcing hailstorms with fire and blood descending, volcanic eruptions, blood in the sea, blight on the land, the pollution of springs and fountains, eclipses of sun and moon with shooting stars, climaxed by an enormous plague of demonic locusts.

These seven angels are identified as "the seven angels who stand before God" (8:2). By this is meant not merely the angels who happened to be standing before the throne, but the seven who, according to Jewish tradition, formed a special group and were distinguished above the rest. This differentiation of the seven appears clearly in the apocryphal book of Tobit, written during the intertestamental period, "I am Raphael, one of the seven angels who stand ready and enter before the glory of the Lord" (Tob. 12:15). The names of the other six, according to the Greek text of the book of Enoch (chapter 20), are Uriel, Raguel, Michael, Sariel, Gabriel, and Remiel. These are the angels that John sees being given trumpets that will figure in the following series of judgments. The trumpet is the favorite instrument of apocalyptists since it summons people's attention to God's communication.

Thereupon the angels put their trumpets to their lips, "ready to blow them" (8:6). Like the opening of the seven seals (6:1–8:4), the sounding of the seven trumpets falls into two groups of four and three. John's description of the series of God's judgments corresponds in some measure to that of the ten plagues sent against the Egyptians in order to persuade Pharaoh to let the people of Israel go (Exod. 7–10). The treatment of Christians by Rome can be compared to the enslavement of the Israelites in Egypt, and God's judgment on the enemies of the church will be like the plagues on the land and people of ancient Egypt.

The last of the four horsemen had authority to harm a fourth of the earth (6:8). At the sounding of the first trumpet the destruction becomes more pervasive, for now one-third is affected (8:7). With the second, third, and fourth trumpets there is a continuation of the affliction of the earth in terms of one-third: sea, sea creatures, ships, rivers, sun, moon, stars, fountains of water. At each of the four trumpets, three things have been touched after their sounding (8:7-12). Obviously John finds some significance in the numbers three, four, and twelve.

The imagery that John uses to describe his visions may have been in part suggested by storms, earthquakes, and eclipses of the first century. If, as is likely, Revelation was written after A.D. 79, when the sudden eruption of Vesuvius completely engulfed the city of Pompeii with molten lava and destroyed ships in the Gulf of Naples, then John's readers, from reports they had heard of the catastrophe, would have had no difficulty picturing "something like a great mountain, burning with fire, [being] thrown into the sea" (8:8).

The judgments that follow each of the first four trumpets are elemental forces of nature, which are directed against the cosmos and which affect humanity indirectly. The last three trumpets call forth demonic forces, falling directly on humanity. They are introduced by an eagle, circling high in mid-heaven and crying out, "Woe, woe, woe to the inhabitants of the earth, at the blasts of the other trumpets that the three angels are about to blow!" (8:13). This announcement of foreboding warns the reader that worse things are to follow.

As in the sequence of the seals, so in the sequence of the trumpets the fifth and sixth are described at greater length than the first four. When the fifth angel blows his trumpet, a plague of demonic locusts is released from the bottomless pit (9:3). The leader of these demonic hordes is Abaddon, the destroyer. Lest the reader fail to grasp the significance of the Hebrew name, John adds the Greek equivalent, Apollyon. As king of the demonic locusts, his mission is to destroy (9:11). Unlike any other swarm of locusts, these are like cavalry horses armed for battle. They have human faces, they wear gold crowns, their hair is like women's hair, their teeth are like lions' teeth, and they have tails with poisonous stings like scorpions (9:7-10). Certainly John's powers of description amaze us!

The mission of these demonic tormentors is not, as might be supposed at first sight, to harm the vegetation on earth; in fact, they are forbidden to do that (9:4). Their attack is to be launched against the oppressors of the Christians for a period of five months (9:5), the usual life-cycle of certain species of natural locusts. Just as the Israelites had been exempt from the plagues of Egypt, so now the Christians who have God's seal upon their foreheads will be completely unharmed by these awful creatures of divine judgment (9:4).

So great will be the suffering caused by the locusts that people prefer death to the agony of living. But death will elude them, and in any case physical death is no remedy for the torment of an evil conscience (9:6).

Then the sixth angel blows his trumpet (9:13) and summons a vast host of horsemen, two hundred million in number, to cross the Euphrates River and to kill a third of humankind. The Euphrates is significant as the eastern frontier of the Roman Empire, beyond which lay the Parthian menace. These demon-horsemen with their mounts, hitherto held in leash, are now let loose like avenging furies upon the Roman provinces at "the hour, the day, the month, and the year" appointed (9:15). The horses of the invaders are frightful, supernatural agents of destruction. They kill people by the fire, smoke, and sulfur issuing from their mouths, and poison them by their tails, which are like the heads of scorpions (9:17-19).

We must remember that the objects and events seen in a vision are not physically real. As was mentioned earlier (pp. 12-13), Ezekiel's vision of the valley of dry bones (Ezek. 37) and Peter's vision of a great sheet let down from heaven and filled with all kinds of unclean creatures (Acts 10) were perceived in a trance. Such things seen in a vision are not physically present. So too, in the book of Revelation the descriptions are not descriptions of real occurrences, but of symbols of the real occurrences. The intention is to fix the reader's thought, not upon the symbol, but upon the idea that the symbolic language is designed to convey.

Dire though the imagery is, the overall intention of the sounding of the seven trumpets is not to inflict vengeance but to bring people to repentance. Although nothing is done to minimize the gravity of sin and rebellion against God, there is great emphasis on God's patience and mercy. Instead of total destruction, only a third (9:18) or some other fraction of the whole is affected. The fraction is symbolic of the mercy of God. The calamity is not universal but leaves those who can learn from tragic events.

It would be natural to think that the remainder of humanity would have taken warning from such dreadful portents. But they do not; they brazenly refuse all opportunity to turn back to God (9:20-21). It is because of their continued stubbornness that pressure on the wicked is progressively increased. With a keen eye to the basic wrong in human nature, John identifies the sin to which the survivors cling so tenaciously:

Idolatry! No doubt for John this involved emperor worship, but whatever its form in that age or in any other age, the worship of any but God alone is always the greatest evil.

Between the sounding of the sixth and seventh trumpets there is another pause (10:1–11:14). Just as there was an interlude before the breaking of the seventh seal, so now there is an interlude before the sounding of the seventh trumpet (11:15). This vision, however, differs from the message of consolation and assurance introduced between the breaking of the sixth and seventh seals. That emphasized the safety and the glory of the persecuted people of God; this message describes the mingling of the sweet and the bitter. It speaks of persecution and tribulation, but also of loyalty and devotion.

The purpose of the interlude in each of the cycles of seven seems to be largely dramatic. With the completion of the sixth in each series we hold our breath in anticipation of the end. But this dramatic writer does not allow the end to come with such rapidity. Each time he makes us wait before we see the seventh of the series. During the first part of this interlude yet another entire cycle of seven is thrown on the screen momentarily and then removed after only a glance has been permitted. The effect is tantalizing. This cycle, which involved seven thunders, was clearly witnessed by the writer, and he was about to write what he had seen when he was told, "seal up what the seven thunders have said, and do not write it down" (10:4). Whether this is again a device used only for effect, or whether it has some deeper significance, it is hard to say. Perhaps the seven thunders were for John what the things that Paul saw in the third heaven were for him. At that time Paul heard, he says, "things that are not to be told, that no mortal is permitted to repeat" (2 Cor. 12:4). This suggests that there are dimensions of reality that mortals are not able to comprehend.

In John's vision he sees "another mighty angel coming down from heaven, wrapped in a cloud, with a rainbow over his head" (10:1)—which means that he is clothed with God's power and mercy. The angel is holding a little scroll open in his hand, and John is told to "take it, and eat"—a way of saying that he is to "read, learn, mark, and inwardly digest," even as we still speak of "devouring a book," meaning that we read it with eagerness. This scroll, which is not the sealed scroll of chapter 5, is a special message from God to John. In his mouth the scroll is sweet as honey, but in his stomach it is bitter (10:10), signifying that it is sweet to him to receive God's message, but that its wrath and judgment fill him with sorrow. Having assimilated the contents of the little scroll, John is commanded to make them known by prophesying "to many peoples and nations and languages and kings" (10:11).

What follows in chapter 11 has been generally acknowledged to be one of the most perplexing sections of the entire book. There is presented here an almost bewildering interweaving of symbols suggested by Old Testament history and prophecy. We find reference to the temple and the altar, to Moses and Elijah, to the wild olive trees and the lampstand seen by Zechariah, to the plagues sent upon Pharaoh, to the tyrant predicted by Daniel, and to Sodom and Egypt and Jerusalem. Perhaps the most that can be said with confidence is that the author views the people of God as bearing faithful testimony, but also as suffering pain and persecution and indignity. They are delivered not *from* martyrdom and death, but *through* martyrdom and death to a glorious resurrection. Nevertheless, beyond such a very general understanding of the passage, some features of Revelation 11:1-14 can be clarified by the patient expositor who seeks to discriminate between what is to be understood literally and what is to be understood symbolically.

How should we take John's statement when he says that he was given a measuring rod and told to "measure the temple of God and the altar and those who worship there" (11:1)? This certainly cannot refer to the Jewish temple in Jerusalem, for when John is writing in the 90s it had been lying in ruins for some twenty years after the Roman armies under Titus had sacked the city in A.D. 70. There is no longer an altar and, of course, no one could measure (that is, count) those who worship there.

Consequently, it appears that here John is using symbolic language and speaks of the temple, not as a building, but as God's people. Measuring is done in order to build and repair, and John is given a measuring rod so that he can restore and revive the church.

Such a spiritualized use of the word *temple* to represent the Christian church is found elsewhere in the New Testament. The apostle Paul, for example, asks the Corinthian believers, "Do you not know that you are God's temple?" (1 Cor. 3:16). Later, he says directly, "We are the temple of the living God" (2 Cor. 6:16). Furthermore, according to Peter, Christians are living stones, built into a spiritual house (1 Pet. 2:5). Thus, the whole church is growing "into a holy temple in the Lord" (Eph. 2:21).

John is told to measure only the inner court of the temple: "Do not measure the court outside the temple . . . for it is given over to the nations" (11:2). Those on the outside are the persecutors of the church, who "will trample over the holy city for forty-two months." They are not only permitted to destroy the church, but are also permitted to oppress it for a limited time. This period (three and a half years) is the traditional apocalyptic term of Gentile domination, derived from Daniel 9:27 and 12:7, where its primary reference is to the time of defilement of the temple by the "abomination that desolates" set up by Antiochus IV from 167 to 164 B.C. This period of time (forty-two months) is 1,260 days during which two witnesses exercise their ministry (11:3). Who are these two witnesses? John offers two different hints as to their identity. The reference to "the two olive trees" (11:4) suggests that he was thinking of Zechariah's vision (Zech. 4:1-14) of Joshua and Zerubbabel. On the other hand, what he says about their authority "to shut the sky, so that no rain may fall" and to turn water into blood (11:6) brings to mind Elijah (2 Kings 1:10) and Moses (Exod. 7:17, 19).

When the two witnesses "have finished their testimony," they are attacked and killed by the beast from the bottomless pit (11:7); this demonic monster will be described in greater detail in chapters 13 and 17. The martyrdom of the two witnesses is likened to that of Christ in Jerusalem ("the great city that is allegorically called Sodom and Egypt" (11:8 margin). Sodom symbolizes moral degradation (Gen. 19:4-11), and Egypt stands for oppression and slavery. The bodies of the witnesses "lie in the street of the great city . . . for three and a half days" (11:8-9). To deny proper burial was considered a great disgrace and insult to the dead.

Although the ministry of the witnesses was exercised in Jerusalem, as the allegory develops, the vision is enlarged to include the entire world. From all parts of the earth, "members of the peoples and tribes and languages and nations" (11:9) celebrate because the two prophets are dead and can no longer vex their conscience by calling sinners to repentance. But God intervenes amid their gloating, gives his servants resurrection-life, and calls them up to heaven (11:12). The grim aftermath following the assumption of God's witnesses is the judgment of God on the wicked city that killed them (11:13). A destructive earthquake wrecks a tenth of the city and brings death to seven thousand of its inhabitants. Shocked out of their lethargy, those who survive are terrified and give glory to the God of heaven (11:13). How often the blood of martyrs becomes the seed of the church! (Tertullian).

What John is concerned to bring out in this section is that the church, whose lot it is to suffer the persecution of this world, will nevertheless continue to give faithful witness to the truth. By means of symbolism he focuses on the security of the church's true life and the safety of the "temple," which cannot be touched. The violent death of the two witnesses, their resurrection after three and a half days, and their ascension into heaven are to be taken not as historical events, but as symbolic of the resurrection of the church, which though often seeming to be defeated, yet will live.

This section of the book of Revelation closes with the sounding of the last of the seven trumpets (11:15). What startles us is that what follows is so utterly unlike anything that the other trumpets announced. It is quite unique that here, instead of such things as volcanic eruptions, demonic locusts, and fire-breathing monsters, we listen to an outburst of rejoicing in heaven. John hears the heavenly chorus celebrating victory: " The kingdom of the world has become the kingdom of our Lord and of his Messiah, and he will reign forever and ever" (11:15).

Following this outburst of praise there comes a response from the twenty-four elders. They celebrate God's assumption of power, his overthrow of the raging nations, his judgment of the dead, and his rewarding of the faithful (11:16-18). Suddenly the song sinks into silence and there bursts on John's sight a new vision of divine glory: "God's temple in heaven was opened" (11:19), revealing the ark of the covenant, the sign of God's presence with his people. The issue of all the judgments, the essence of all the rewards, is to have a more perfect access to God and a clearer vision of his splendor.

Certainly this has all the appearance of the end of the age, with judgment of the dead and rewarding of the saints and all who fear God's name, both small and great (11:18). If John had finished his book here, we would have considered it properly terminated. But since there are eleven more chapters, the author will now go back to an earlier stage and repeat some of the teachings that he had previously set before the reader. Thus, we see here confirmation of the comment made in the opening chapter (p. 21 above): the sequence in which John's visions are presented does not allow us to turn the book of Revelation into an almanac or time chart of the last days.[1]

---

1. On the "last days" see p. 95 below.

8

THE SATANIC TRINITY: THE DRAGON AND THE TWO BEASTS

(Revelation 12:1–14:20)

CHAPTER 11 of the book of Revelation concludes with references to judging the dead, rewarding the servants of God, and opening God's temple in heaven. Although this scenario would make a fitting end of the book, John has still more to reveal to the reader. To present this further material he returns to an earlier stage and, so to speak, begins all over again. Chapter 12 can be characterized as a flashback, telling of the birth of the Messiah and the attempt of King Herod to kill Jesus soon after he was born. However, instead of telling this as a historical narrative in a straightforward manner as Matthew does (Matt. 2), John presents a heavenly tableau of characters that are portrayed with sensational Near Eastern imagery. In describing the tableau John borrows old apocalyptic motifs, some of which have their roots in a dim and distant past. Striking parallels have been found in Babylonian, Persian, Egyptian, and Greek mythology, and in astrological lore. The important question, however, is not what sources John may have used, but what use he now makes of them. Because of the unusual kinds of imagery that are combined here, it is not surprising that many readers find this chapter to be one of the most bizarre in the book.

John opens his account with a graphic description of a great portent in heaven. The word *portent*, which occurs here for the first time in his book, marks the beginning of a new series of visions. John sees "a woman clothed with the sun, with the moon under her feet, and on her head a crown of twelve stars" (12:1). She is about to give birth to a child. Meanwhile John's attention is drawn to another great but ominous portent in heaven: "a great red dragon, with seven heads and ten horns" (12:3). Everyone knows that a dragon is fearful enough, but this is a great red dragon! His huge size is suggested by the comment that, while crouching in the sky, a flick of his tail dislodges a third of the stars and sends them hurtling to earth. Then the dragon stands before the woman in order to devour her child as soon as it is born. The woman bears a son, but the child is saved from the dragon by God's intervention.

What does all this signify? Martin Luther once observed in another context that unless people know what is being talked about, they cannot make sense of what is being said. John himself tells us in verse 9 that the dragon represents Satan, the devil. Furthermore, the child is obviously the Christ, for again John provides the key by identifying him as the one "who is to rule all the nations with a rod of iron." These words, taken from Psalm 2:9, were understood by Jews as a prediction of the role of the coming Messiah. The dragon's eagerness to devour the child explains the violent opposition that Jesus met during his earthly ministry. It began with the slaughter of the children in Bethlehem (Matt. 2:16) and culminated when he was crucified outside the city of Jerusalem.

Satan, however, is thwarted. The child is "snatched away and taken to God and to his throne" (12:5)—a reference to the Ascension. Here the gospel story is surprisingly condensed, but enough is said to accomplish John's purpose. He has shown the deadly enmity of the Adversary, his defeat, and the exaltation of Christ to the place of supreme and universal power.

The woman, clothed with the sun, standing on the moon, and wearing a crown of stars, has been variously interpreted

73

by some as the Virgin Mary, by others as the Christian church, and by still others as the Jewish people. What John probably intended was a personification of the ideal community of God's people, first in its Jewish form, in which Mary gave birth to Jesus the Messiah, and then in its Christian form, in which it was persecuted by a political power as evil as the dragon (12:6).

In the next scene the dragon, apparently angered by his failure to kill the newborn Messiah, engages in war with Michael and his angels (12:7-9). The archangel Michael was regarded as the heavenly patron of Israel (Dan. 10:13, 21; 12:1), and so, by extension, of the new people of God. Michael defeats the dragon and casts him out of heaven down to earth. The dragon's defeat and eviction from heaven are the cause of great rejoicing by the remaining heavenly dwellers (12:10-12). In Christ's victory, the victory of his people is included:

> "They have conquered him [the devil] by
> the blood of the Lamb
> and by the word of their
> testimony,
> for they did not cling to life even
> in the face of death.
> Rejoice then, you heavens
> and those who dwell in them!" (12:11-12*a*)

The words of the triumph song remind us that the vision of Michael fighting the dragon is symbolic, representing the real victory won by the atoning death of Christ and the preaching of the gospel.

The last verses of the chapter show Satan's persistent hostility against the church and his persecution of the faithful. Obviously, John uses metaphorical language (the earth has no "mouth," verse 16), but the truths he communicates through symbols are as real as if they had been told in

74

nonmetaphorical terms. In furious wrath the dragon begins to inflict great harm on the other children of the woman (12:17)—that is, on Christians who obey God and bear testimony to Jesus. By this retrospective tableau the author explains how the persecution of Christians began. He charges the devil with the primary responsibility for initiating it. In the following chapter (13) two of Satan's agents appear. These two, along with the dragon, comprise a counterfeit trinity. One is a frightful beast, rising out of the sea, who is given power by the dragon. This beast symbolizes the Roman Empire, which in John's day was the embodiment of Antichrist, a world power in opposition to the reign of Christ. The beast, we are told, "opened its mouth to utter blasphemies against God" (13:6), reviling his name and his heavenly dwelling. We know what this means. Beginning with Julius Caesar, Roman emperors had been deified, that is, were given the status and worship due to a god, the early ones after their death, but later emperors even during their lifetime. As was mentioned earlier, the Emperor Domitian required that people address him as "our lord and god." In most of the cities to which John was writing, temples had been built to these "deities"—a mockery of the heavenly dwelling of the one true God.

Although this policy of promoting an emperor-cult came ultimately from the emperor himself, its execution lay in the hands of local officials. These political underlings could be aptly represented by the second beast that John saw coming up out of the earth (13:11) and whom he later calls the false prophet (16:13). This is personified paganism itself. With a grim parody John describes the beast as having "two horns like a lamb"—that is, it has taken on the guise of God's chosen one, yet "it spoke like a dragon" (13:11). This agent of the dragon promoted the worship of the emperor by means of all kinds of spectacular tricks of bogus religion (13:13-15), even causing the image of the first beast to appear to be alive. One of the ways a ruler impressed his sovereignty most vividly on the minds of his subjects was by issuing coins bearing his image and title. Throughout the Roman Empire, every transaction of buying and selling, if it involved the transfer of money, meant handling imperial coins. Around the head of the emperor on a coin were titles, including in some cases references to his being divine and worshipful. It is such coins that John refers to as bearing the mark of the beast, without which "no one can buy or sell" (13:17). Consequently, resistance by Christians to the cult of the emperor would entail the very worst consequences—being subject to economic problems as well as to persecution.

The details of John's vision are symbolic. Thus, the "mark" on the right hand or the forehead (13:16) is meant figuratively. Those who conform to the demands of the state are given means to identify themselves, so that they can claim the benefits due to them.

The famous "number of the beast" is mentioned at the end of chapter 13. The number "six hundred sixty-six" is, in the first place, a symbol of the greatest imperfection, for it is the sacred number seven less one, repeated thrice. John says that it is a human number, that is, it is the number of a person's name. Now, in both the Greek and the Hebrew alphabets, the letters also served as numerals, and it was a well-known technique to add up the letters that comprise a proper name. If we did that in English, the number of a girl named Ada would be 6. That is, A is the first letter of the alphabet and D is the fourth letter, and consequently the numerical equivalent of Ada is $1 + 4 + 1 = 6$.

Who is this satanic beast, symbolized by the number 666? Over the centuries a very great deal of ingenuity has been expended in attempting to answer this question. A further complication arises from the fact that some ancient manuscripts of the book of Revelation give the number as 616 instead of 666.

Among the names and titles that have been proposed to solve the cryptogram, the most probable candidate is the

Emperor Nero. If we add the numerical values in the Hebrew[1] spelling of the name Neron Caesar we obtain 666; on the other hand, since his name can equally well be spelled without the last N, if we omit the final N, the total will be 616. There does not appear to be any other name, or a name with a title, that satisfies both 666 and 616.

The profound religious insight that lies behind these kaleidoscopic pictures in chapter 13 is that men and women are so constituted as to worship some absolute power, and if they do not worship the true and real Power behind the universe, they will construct a god for themselves and give allegiance to that. In the last analysis, it is always a choice between the power that operates through inflicting suffering, that is, the power of the beast, and the power that operates through accepting suffering, namely, the power of the Lamb.

Following the account of the counterfeit trinity, John once again provides an interlude that is intended to reassure the church amid its trials and persecutions. We have noticed before that one of the characteristics of this book is the alternation of sharp contrasts between scenes of frightful horror and scenes of welcome security. The first part of chapter 14 is a scene of tranquility and rejoicing. John sees the Lamb, standing on Mount Zion, with the 144,000 of the redeemed. As was mentioned earlier (p. 61), 144,000 is a symbolic number, representing all those who remain faithful. Here an added comment is made: "It is these who have not defiled themselves with women, for they are virgins" (14:4). On the surface this means that only men who have never had sexual intercourse can "follow the Lamb wherever he goes." Since, however, the rest of the Bible sanctions and commends

---

1. In the Hebrew alphabet (which consists of consonants only), the tenth letter has the numerical value of 10, but the eleventh letter represents 20, and the following letters carry on by tens until 100. Thereafter, the letters carry on by hundreds (200, and so on). Thus, the "full" spelling of "Nero Caesar" in Hebrew letters is N, R, W, N, Q, S, R. These letters have the following numerical values: N = 50, R = 200, W = 6, N = 50, Q = 100, S = 60, and R = 200.

marriage, one hesitates to understand this as a condemnation of marriage or a demand for celibacy. Rather, John appears to adopt the imagery found frequently in the Old Testament where any contact with pagan worship was called "fornication" or "adultery." Hence, the 144,000 are those who have not defiled themselves by participating in pagan worship.

Next John sees an "angel flying in midheaven, with an eternal gospel to proclaim to those who live on the earth" (14:6). The angel says in a loud voice, "Fear God and give him glory, for the hour of his judgment has come; and worship him who made heaven and earth, the sea and the springs of water" (14:7).

Another angel announces the fall of Babylon (14:8), a theme that John will take up later in great detail (chapter 19). These two angels are followed by a third who predicts eternal condemnation for those who persist in worshiping the beast and its image. Such people, he declares, will "drink the wine of God's wrath . . . and they will be tormented with fire and sulfur. . . . And the smoke of their torment goes up forever and ever. There is no rest day or night for those who worship the beast and its image" (14:10-11).

This passage gives offense to some modern readers of Revelation; certainly it sounds terribly vindictive and gruesome. But the first thing to do is to consider the symbolic language used here. Fire and brimstone are traditional symbols for the fate of those who persistently reject God. (Brimstone is an Old English term for sulfur, which is not only difficult to extinguish, but also burns with peculiarly acrid and noxious fumes.) Since elsewhere in the book of Revelation the author uses metaphors and symbolic language, it would be quite unfair to take him literally here. Now throughout Revelation we have seen that if people persist in living contrary to the structure of God's universe, they must suffer. John's words here mean that the most terrible thing that a person can do is deliberately to turn away from the living God. Such torment, says John, is "forever and ever." This is so, because

God respects our free will and will never force us to turn to him. So this picture of wrath and hell means nothing more or less than the terrible truth that the sufferings of those who persist in rejecting God's love in Christ are self-imposed and self-perpetuated. The inevitable consequence is that if they eternally persist in such rejection, God will never violate their personality. Whether any soul will in fact eternally resist God, we cannot say.

These solemn thoughts are followed by words of comfort, which comprise the second of the seven beatitudes contained in the book of Revelation. John hears a voice from heaven declaring, "Blessed are the dead who from now on die in the Lord." "Yes," says the Spirit, "they will rest from their labors, for their deeds follow them" (14:13). Their good deeds and patient sufferings will follow them as witnesses for them before the Judge of the living and the dead (see pp. 95-96 below).

9

THE SEVEN BOWLS OF GOD'S WRATH

(Revelation 15:1–18:24)

THE writer of the book of Revelation has carefully laid out a series of parallel and yet ever-progressing panels. These display God's plan from different vantage points, stressing one or another feature. At the same time, the different accounts reinforce one another and bring before the reader, over and over again, the truth that God rules and overrules in the affairs of humankind.

In chapters 15 through 18 the struggle of the church in its conflict with hostile world powers reaches new levels of intensity. Earlier in chapter 6 we were told of the opening of the seven seals (pp. 55-62), followed in chapters 8 and 9 by the seven trumpets announcing additional woes (pp. 63-67). Now in chapters 15 and 16 we come to an account of the seven bowls full of God's wrath poured successively by each of the seven angels on the earth, on the sea, on the rivers and fountains, on the sun, on the throne of the beast, on the great River Euphrates, and finally into the air (16:2-17). These are described as "seven plagues, which are the last, for with them the wrath of God is ended" (15:1). They are the last or final cycle of visitations, bringing to a close God's warnings to the impenitent.

Prior to the opening of the seventh seal (8:1-2), which introduced the seven trumpet woes, John portrayed the security of God's faithful by telling of the 144,000 that had been sealed and the great multitude in white robes (pp. 60-62 above). Now, before describing the seven plagues of divine wrath, John portrays the safety of "those who had conquered the beast and its image and the number of its name" (15:2). These victors, with harps of God in their hands, "sing the song of Moses . . . and the song of the Lamb" (15:3). In Exodus 15:1-18, the words of the song of Moses after crossing the Red Sea are very different from those of the song of the Lamb, and John is not suggesting that they were the same song. But both celebrate deliverance from deadly danger.

The song expresses confidence that all nations will be led to worship the one true God, because they will acknowledge the justice of what he has done in vindicating his people. As the seer listens to the song, it swells into an anthem that celebrates the mercies of the Lord God. The song consists almost entirely of echoes from various parts of the Old Testament—showing once again how thoroughly John's thought had been shaped by the Scriptures. The structure of the song reflects the parallelism characteristic of Hebrew poetry.

> "Great and amazing are your
>   deeds,
>   Lord God the Almighty!
> Just and true are your ways,
>   King of the nations!
> Lord, who will not fear
>   and glorify your name?
> For you alone are holy.
>   All nations will come
>   and worship before you,
> for your judgments have been
>   revealed." (15:3-4)

One of the most striking features of this song of the triumphant martyrs is the absence of any mention of their own victory and their own achievement. From beginning to end

81

the whole song is a lyrical outburst celebrating the greatness of God. The hymn itself, like other songs in Revelation, may have been used in the early church. They make some of our modern ephemeral ditties appear incredibly trite.

Following the victors' song of praise, John sees that "the temple of the tent of witness in heaven was opened" (15:5), and out of it came seven angels, "robed in pure bright linen,[1] with golden sashes across their chests. Then one of the four living creatures gave the seven angels seven golden bowls full of the wrath of God" (15:6-7). The Greek word for "bowls" denotes vessels that are broad and shallow, shaped like a saucer, so that their contents can be poured out completely and suddenly.

John then hears a loud voice from the temple telling the seven angels, "Go and pour out on the earth the seven bowls of the wrath of God" (16:1). This destruction is directed against those "who had the mark of the beast and who worshiped its image" (16:2). Thereupon the bowls of God's wrath are emptied. This succession of plagues is not to be understood as an orgy of indiscriminate destruction, but as the working out of God's justice in judgment upon those who worship the beast. The repeated emphasis on their lack of repentance indicates their true allegiance insofar as they blaspheme the living God (16:9 and 11).

The author's descriptive details of the plagues are not to be taken literally, but as contributing to the general effect of intense calamity and terror. As was mentioned earlier, the descriptions are descriptions of the symbols, not of the reality conveyed by the symbols. The justice of God must bring judgment upon individuals and upon nations that violate the moral structure of God's universe. Like a good teacher, John repeats with kaleidoscopic variety his central conviction that God rules and overrules in the affairs of the church and the

---

1. Some ancient manuscripts have "robed in pure bright stone" because scribes misread the Greek word *linon* as *lithon*.

world. We might say that John sets up several mirrors in which the same objects are reflected from different sides, so that the reader cannot fail to take note of them.

At the same time, there does seem to be a certain progression. The seventh in each of the first two series of woes produces another series, similar to the previous series but more terrible. Following the opening of the seals, the second series of trumpets ushers in new disasters, which are blasts of warning, calling men and women to repentance. By the time of the third series, the summons to repentance having proved to be unheeded, further judgments are poured out from the bowls of God's wrath—a picture of swift, uninterrupted, and complete punishment.

John's motive for such repetition of woes appears to have been a desire to prepare the church for a period of suffering. Although he is confident that the Lord will come soon and bring deliverance, he does not want to delude his readers with hopes that may be premature. Nothing in the book is more remarkable than the grim honesty with which the writer faces the situation before him. Of course he desires to comfort his fellow-sufferers, but he does not comfort them with any false hopes. Fully conscious of the calamities that await it, the church must prepare to meet them undaunted.

The literary artistry with which the man of Patmos has constructed his book is particularly evident in the long middle section (6:1–16:21). In order to relieve the monotony of a succession of calamities and woes, John provides an interlude that follows each of the three series of judgments. In addition, within each series he has made room for songs of praise as well as expressions of lamentation. With all its seeming confusion, the book has an overall unity, and the skill with which it is woven together can be seen particularly in this middle section.

It is also in this section that the author refers to what is commonly called the battle of Armageddon. When the sixth angel has emptied his bowl of doom, a strange and unusual happening takes place (16:13). A foul spirit like a frog comes from the mouth of the dragon, another from the mouth of the first beast, and a third from the mouth of the second beast, identified here as the false prophet. These foul spirits, pictured as demonic frogs more dreadful than those of the Egyptian plague of frogs in the time of Moses (Exod. 8:2-14), perform signs in an attempt to deceive the kings of the earth. The frogs and their croaking represent generally the ability to deceive by means of superstitions, preposterous claims, and lies. Propaganda, unscrupulously used by totalitarian states, would certainly be a modern illustration of this picture. John sees these demonic spirits as going abroad in order to assemble the kings of the whole world for a battle that is to occur at a place called Armageddon (16:16).

This mouth-filling word, like the number 666, has been magnified in popular thinking out of all proportion to its significance as a word. Curiously enough, no one knows for certain what the name Armageddon means. First, we do not really know how to spell it. In some Greek manuscripts of Revelation it is spelled Harmagedon. The scribes of other manuscripts spell the word with one *d* and two *g*'s; others with two *d*'s and one *g*; others still with two *g*'s and two *d*'s. In spite of the difficulty of knowing how to spell the word, and consequently what it means and where the place is located, most scholars suppose that it alludes to the mountain of Megiddo. The difficulty with this, however, is that there is no "Mount Megiddo"; Megiddo was the name of a city that gave its name to the pass between the coastal plains of Palestine and the Plain of Esdraelon. Because this had been the scene of frequent and decisive battles in ancient times (Judg. 5:19-21; 2 Kings 9:27; 23:29), it would appear that John is using familiar language to symbolize the final great conflict between the forces of good and the forces of evil, a battle in which evil will be defeated—not by armaments but by God's incarnate Word, Jesus Christ (19:13).

Finally, the seventh angel pours out his bowl (16:17) and a

mighty voice out of the heavenly temple cries, "It is done!" Judgment day for Babylon has arrived (16:19). Amid natural catastrophes of unprecedented ferocity, Babylon falls. The seven plagues end with a bombardment of massive hailstones, each weighing about a hundred pounds (16:21).

Chapters 17 and 18 are a literary triumph of imaginative power. More than once John had found comfort for himself and his people by proclaiming the fall of Rome. So certain is he that God will judge the persecutors of the church that he now devotes two chapters to an account of the crashing down of the fabulous "grandeur that was Rome." To say directly that God will destroy imperial Rome would have been, of course, altogether treasonous in the eyes of the imperial authorities. So, like a prisoner writing in code from a concentration camp, John characterizes the power of evil as Babylon. Just as Babylon represented to the Hebrews all that was wicked and symbolized persecution, so for John Rome was another Babylon, the source and fountainhead of all seductive luxury and vice, living in voluptuous materialism and selfishness.

Here John paints a picture of Rome in colors highly figurative and repellent. "Look at her," says John, "that whore among cities, the courtesan of the world." Dressed in purple and scarlet, she is resplendent and seductive, "adorned with gold and jewels and pearls" (17:4). Instead of having a scepter in her hand, she is holding a golden cup that is filled with the impurities of her fornications, the abominations of her idolatries. Seated on a scarlet beast that is covered with blasphemous names, the woman personifies imperial power and oppression. The statement that "the kings of the earth have committed fornication" with her (17:2) must be understood metaphorically to mean that Rome has usurped and perverted the political power of all her provinces. She is drunk, not with wine, but with the lifeblood of the martyrs of Jesus whom she caused to be slain (17:6).

The reference here is to wild orgies of persecution, such as those instigated by Nero and described by the Roman historian Tacitus. According to that non-Christian writer, in the 60s of the first century, "a vast multitude of Christians were not only put to death, but put to death with insult. They were either clothed in the skins of wild beasts and then exposed in the arena to the attacks of half-famished dogs, or else dipped in tar and put on crosses to be set on fire, and, when the daylight failed, to be burned as lights by night" (*Annals* XV, 44). Tacitus comments that Nero's persecution of Christians was so terrible that even non-Christian citizens were horrified and began to intercede in their behalf.

In chapter 18 John describes the fall of Rome with pathos and realism. The literature of the world contains few passages that compare in dramatic power with this dirge over the fallen city. Like the tolling of a funeral bell, we hear the repeated lamentation: "Alas, alas, the great city!" (18:10, 16, 19). Despite all her sins and crimes, there are many who mourn for her. The kings of the earth who had consorted with her "weep and wail over her when they see the smoke of her burning" (18:9). The merchants who became wealthy because of her great commerce and trade "weep and mourn for her, since no one buys their cargo anymore" (18:11). And among their merchandise of luxuries as well as necessities there are "slaves—and human lives" (18:13). By mentioning slaves at the end of the list of commodities, John intends a climax: the essential inhumanity of Rome's exploitation of the empire clearly reveals itself by the constant flow of slaves from the provinces to the city of Rome. By John's time slaves made up almost half the population of the city.

The last three words of the list ("and human lives") refer to something even more sinister than the regular slave trade. For, along with the slaves who were the manual and clerical workers in the houses of the great, there were others whose fate was to fight for their lives and to die for the entertainment of the Roman crowds in the amphitheaters built for that purpose by the Caesars. These victims too were among the delicious fruits to which Roman taste had become accustomed (18:14).

The shipmasters and sailors stand far off as the city burns and throw dust on their heads, crying out, "What city was like the great city? . . . For in one hour she has been laid waste." (18:17-19). Here once again (as earlier in 18:9 and 15), John allows us to see the fall of Rome from the perspective of those who had grown powerful and rich through their involvement with the city and its economic system. For such people, of course, Rome's downfall is also their own—no wonder they mourn! But from John's perspective, the fall of Rome is cause for rejoicing and praise of God (18:20; 19:1).

The chapter concludes with a remarkable passage (18:21-24) that describes with haunting power the tragic end of the city. In contrast to her former festivity, the daily activity of her busy artisans, and her domestic labors and joys, now all is silence and desolation and ruin. The dirge concludes (18:24) with the explanation that Rome is to be destroyed because of the blood of prophets and saints whom she has caused to be slaughtered—martyred, it is implied, because they had refused to take part in the cult of the emperor-gods.

It is remarkable that when John wrote these immensely moving chapters about the fall of Rome, Rome was still very much alive, still enjoying undisputed sovereignty and undimmed prestige. So great, however, is John's faith in the sovereignty of God and so great is his confidence that the justice of God must eventually punish evil, that he writes as though Rome had already fallen. As with so many judgments of God, the fulfillment actually came slowly, but at last suddenly. For centuries Rome decayed and degenerated, moral poison infecting her whole life. Then during a fateful week in August of the year A.D. 410, Alaric, with his northern hordes of Goths, pillaged Rome and laid it waste.

What do we learn from this part of the book of Revelation? Certainly John wrote in order to stimulate faithfulness on the part of persecuted Christians living in the first century. He assures them of the ultimate victory of Christ. But Revelation also has a warning for believers down through the years. Babylon is allegorical of the idolatry that any nation commits when it elevates material abundance, military prowess, technological sophistication, imperial grandeur, racial pride, and any other glorification of the creature over the Creator. In these chapters we have an up-to-date portrait of what may occur when we idolize the gross national product, worship growth, and become so preoccupied with quantity that we ignore quality. The message of the book of Revelation concerns the character and timeliness of God's judgment not only of persons, but also of nations and, in fact, of all principalities and powers—which is to say, all authorities, corporations, institutions, structures, bureaucracies, and the like. And, to the extent that ecclesiastical denominations and sects have succumbed to the lure of power and prestige, the words of John are applicable also to present-day church structures.

10

THE FINAL VICTORY AND THE LAST JUDGMENT

(Revelation 19:1–20:15)

I N contrast to the lament and dirges over the fall of
Babylon in the previous chapter, the setting is now
changed to heaven, where the voices of a great multitude are heard singing choruses that begin with "Hallelujah!"[1] (19:1-3). After celebrating the destruction of
the profligate city, Babylon, the larger and more important part of the songs of praise looks to the future, the
perfected union of Christ and his bride, the church. In
this grand oratorio all the choirs of heaven unite. First,
the twenty-four elders and the four living creatures fall
down and worship God, who is seated on the throne,
saying, "Amen. Hallelujah!" (19:4). Then a voice comes
from the throne saying, "Praise our God, all you his
servants, and all that fear him, small and great." This
comprehensive phrase, "small and great," includes believers of all classes and abilities, and of all stages of
progress in their Christian life.

Finally, John hears "what seemed to be the voice of a great
multitude, like the sound of many waters and like the sound

---

1. The word *Hallelujah* transliterates a Hebrew expression that means "Praise Jah,"
that is, "Praise the Lord." It occurs only here in the New Testament (19:1, 3, 4, and
6).

of mighty thunderpeals" (19:6). The heavenly voices trium-
phantly announce:

> "The Lord our God
> the Almighty reigns.
> Let us rejoice and exult
> and give him the glory,
> for the marriage of the Lamb
> has come,
> and his bride has made herself
> ready." (19:6-7)

The concept of the relationship between God and his
people as a marriage goes far back into the Old Testament.
Again and again the prophets spoke of Israel as the chosen
bride of God (Isa. 54:1-8; Ezek. 16:7; Hos. 2:19). In the New
Testament the church is represented as the bride of Christ;
he loved the church so much that he gave himself up in her
behalf (Eph. 5:25). In the words of a familiar hymn: "With his
own blood he bought her, and for her life he died."

As the majestic chorus of praise to God reaches its end,
John hears a voice commanding him to record the fourth of
the seven beatitudes found in the book of Revelation: "Write
this: Blessed are those who are invited to the marriage supper
of the Lamb" (19:9). Mention of the wedding feast of Christ
and his bride, the church, is a signal that the climax of the
drama is very close at hand. Satan is about to be overthrown,
and his dominion is nearing its end. From here on the tempo
of the action increases. The ultimate outcome cannot be in
doubt, but there are some surprises ahead, with the suspense
of the drama sustained to the conclusion.

From verse 11 to the first verse of chapter 21, we have in
rapid succession seven visions preparatory to the end. Each of
these begins with the words "I saw." Out of the opened heaven
there comes into John's view a white horse, symbolic of victory.
Its rider is called "Faithful and True." He has piercing eyes

like a flame of fire (as in 1:14), and on his head are many crowns ("diadems," crowns of royalty). To be crowned with more than one crown may seem a strange picture, but in John's time it was not uncommon for a monarch to wear more than one crown in order to show that he was king of more than one country.

The rider, who is the conquering Christ, "is clothed in a robe dipped in blood" (19:13). This description recalls Isaiah 63:1-3, where the conqueror's garments are stained crimson with the blood of his Edomite enemies. But here John reshapes the imagery to portray the gospel of Christ who triumphed by shedding his own blood (see 5:6 and 9). He is called "The Word of God" (19:13). Christ's proper name is not meant here, but rather his office; it is through him that God has spoken fully and finally to us (see Heb. 1:1-2). Following Christ are "the armies of heaven . . . on white horses"; instead of wearing armor, they are clad in "fine linen, white and pure" (19:14). As in the initial vision of the heavenly Christ (1:16), so too here "from his mouth comes a sharp sword with which to strike down the nations" (19:15). That sword is his word; it is his only armament. By it he convicts, convinces, and exonerates.

John sees "an angel standing in the sun" (19:17) who calls the vultures of the sky to gather at a great feast where they may gorge themselves on the corpses of those who have fallen in battle. The revolting scene is based on the visions of Ezekiel (chapters 38 and 39, especially 39:17-20) when God commands birds of every kind to gather for a feast on the warriors and princes of Gog. John freely adapts Ezekiel's account to his own use both here and in 20:7-10. This carrion meal is obviously a solemn travesty on the marriage supper of the Lamb, an announcement of which has introduced this scene of punishment (19:9).

All this is symbolism at its highest. No one imagines that such statements are literal. Never shall we see the "white horse," or the sword projecting from the mouth of the conqueror, or the birds gorged with the flesh of fallen warriors (19:21). The descriptions are not descriptions of real occurrences, but of symbols of the real occurrences. The message that John conveys through this symbolism is that evil will surely be overthrown. Here that message is presented in apocalyptic pictures of almost repellent realism.

Now the final, great conflict between good and evil takes place. "The beast and the kings of the earth with their armies" (19:19) come face to face with Christ and his followers. This immensely critical moment has been in John's view from the beginning, and we might have expected to read details of how the battle went, with its different phases and critical moments. But the man of Patmos makes no statement about the battle, which is evidence that he intends to describe not an earthly military campaign but a spiritual struggle. He portrays only the result—the overwhelming defeat of the enemies of Christ. The beast is captured along with his chief lieutenant, the false prophet, who has been identified as the Roman religious cult (13:11-18). In the figurative language of apocalyptic, both are "thrown alive into the lake of fire that burns with sulfur" (19:20).

It is noteworthy that the victory is won by Christ's word alone without any military help from the faithful. This picture contrasts sharply with other apocalypses of the period and, in particular, with the War Scroll of the Qumran sect. According to these documents the military help of the faithful is necessary; in fact, the Qumran scroll gives precise directives for the disposition and weapons of the front formations and for the disposition and movements of the cavalry (*War Scroll,* columns 5-6).

Having related the destruction of the beast and the false prophet, John now turns to the ultimate enemy who deceived the nations, identified by four sinister names: the dragon, the ancient serpent, the devil, or Satan. John sees an angel descend from heaven with a chain in his hand and with the key to the bottomless pit (20:1). The angel seizes Satan, binds him with the chain, and locks him in the pit for a thousand years (20:3).

During this period the souls of those who had died a martyr's death because they would not worship the beast come to life and reign with Christ for a thousand years. Whether it is these or another group not otherwise identified that are "given authority to judge" (20:4), John does not say. Nor does he say that Christ and those who come to life return to the earth for these thousand years. In any case, however, John carefully distinguishes the martyrs from all others, going so far as to say that none of the rest of the dead come to life in this millennial blessedness (20:5). Their resurrection appears to be spiritual and not corporeal. A beatitude (the fifth of the seven in Revelation) is pronounced on those who participate in this resurrection (20:6). "The second death has no power" over them (see comment on verse 14), and as "priests of God and of Christ" they will enjoy unimaginable exaltation, security, and blessedness. Their patient endurance of persecution was, by comparison, for only a short time.

After the thousand years Satan is released for a little while (20:3, 7). Just why this is done, and by whom, is an undisclosed mystery. Now Satan resumes his deception of the nations, and instigates two mysterious figures, Gog and Magog, as his obedient tools (20:8). The prophet Ezekiel refers to "Gog, of the land of Magog, the chief prince of Meshech and Tubal" (Ezek. 38:2), who will come from the north against God's people living peacefully in the land. The limited scope of Ezekiel's oracles is expanded in Revelation to cosmic proportions. Whereas in Ezekiel Magog is the territory of which Gog is the ruler, here (as well as in Jewish rabbinic literature) Gog and Magog are parallel names, used together of the world powers opposed to God. It is altogether misguided ingenuity to attempt to identify specific nations today as Gog and Magog, for John says these nations are innumerable (20:8).

With their armies they besiege "the beloved city" (this would be Jerusalem if a literal city is intended). The situation appears to be desperate, but fire quite opportunely comes down from heaven and consumes Gog and Magog and their armies (20:9). Following their defeat, Satan is captured once more, and this time he is thrown into the lake of fire and sulfur, where his cohorts, the beast and the false prophet, had been consigned (see 19:20). Here the unholy trinity "will be tormented day and night forever" (20:10). Satan's rule is now completely and absolutely finished, and his world-age is ended forever.

Such is the account of the thousand-year period in chapter 20 of Revelation—the only place in the Bible that mentions the millennium. The word *millennium* is a Latin term that means one thousand years. Over the centuries diverse interpretations have been built on these few verses. Commentators have read into John's account ideas from other parts of the Bible (such as the rapture, the tribulation, the reconstruction of the Jewish temple), none of which are mentioned here. Such elaborations generally fall into one of three principal schools of interpretation.

1. Postmillennialists believe that Christ will come after the millennium has taken place. The kingdom of God is now being extended in the world through the preaching of the gospel and the saving work of the Holy Spirit. Christ is already reigning through his obedient church, and will bring to the world a thousand years of peace and righteousness prior to his return at the conclusion of history.

2. Premillennialists maintain that Christ will come before the millennium begins. Despite all attempts to Christianize society, things will become worse and worse, and in the last days Antichrist will gain control of human affairs. Only the catastrophic return of Christ can inaugurate the golden age of one thousand years of peace here on earth.

3. Amillennialists regard the thousand years, like other numerals in Revelation, to be symbolic. Instead of being a literal period of exactly one thousand years, the expression refers to a very long time, extending from the first coming of

Christ to his Second Coming. During this entire period Satan's power is limited by the preaching of the gospel (Luke 10:18). The "last days" began with Jesus (Heb. 1:2) and with the outpouring of the Holy Spirit on the day of Pentecost (Acts 2:16, 17), and they will end when the "last day" arrives (John 6:39, 40, 44, 54; 11:24; 12:48). Instead of the optimism of the postmillenarian or the pessimism of the premillenarian, the amillenarian takes seriously the realism of Jesus' parable of the weeds among the wheat (Matt. 13:24-30, 36-43), namely, that good and evil will develop side by side until the harvest, which is at the end of the world.

Each of these interpretations involves various difficulties,[2] but the central truth of all three is the clear and direct affirmation: Christ will return, as he had promised (John 14:3), and will destroy the forces of evil and establish God's eternal kingdom.

John's next vision is one of awesome and sobering impressiveness; it is a vision of the Last Judgment (20:11-15). He sees a great white throne—it is great because it is God's throne, and it is white because of God's eternal purity. Next a most astounding thing occurs: the earth and the heaven, John says, "fled from [God's] presence, and no place was found for them" (20:11). That is, the one seated on the throne is so radiant and consuming that earth and sky vanish like dew in the sun. Then all the dead, without respect of persons, are brought before the judgment seat of God. " The great and the small," that is, those who were important and those who were unimportant in this life, are assembled together; there are no absentees and there are no exemptions. Next John tells us that

---

2. For discussions of what can be said for and against each of the main views of the millennium, see Robert H. Clouse, *The Meaning of the Millennium: Four Views* (Downers Grove, Ill.: InterVarsity Press, 1979); Stanley J. Grenz, *The Millennial Maze: Sorting Out Evangelical Options* (Downers Grove, Ill.: InterVarsity Press, 1992); and for a comprehensive discussion of the history of the interpretation of Revelation, see Arthur W. Wainwright, *Mysterious Apocalypse: Interpreting the Book of Revelation* (Nashville: Abingdon Press, 1993).

books are opened. One book can be called the Book of Merit, for it contains a record and remembrance of all the deeds of each one who stands before the throne of God. Another book is the book of life, which belongs to the Lamb (13:8; 21:27); this can be called the Book of Mercy. Here the work of Christ, who died to ransom his people and save them from their sin, is put on the credit side of the ledger, along with the names of all who are destined for acquittal and blessedness.

That books will be consulted in the final judgment is an idea found in many ancient traditions. Besides nonbiblical sources,[3] the conception of a heavenly register of the elect is mentioned in various parts of the Old Testament (for example, Exod. 32:32-33; Ps. 69:28; Dan. 7:10; Mal. 3:16). While we cannot conceive of actual books being written to record our lives, there is a sense in which the term *books* carries a deep and significant meaning. John obviously found the symbolism of the book of life to be suggestive, for he refers to it five times throughout Revelation (3:5; 13:8; 17:8; 20:12, 15; and 21:27).[4]

The giving up of the dead by "the sea" and by "Death and Hades" signifies that all the dead are raised and brought to judgment. The manner and the place of dying make no difference; all are judged "according to what they had done" (20:13)—for there is no other way that judgment can be rendered (see 1 Cor. 3:11-15). Finally the two great enemies of humankind—Death and Hades, which are here personified—are destroyed after giving up the dead that were in them (20:13). These voracious monsters that devour mortals are now overcome and have no more power over humankind (compare 6:8). They are thrown into the lake of fire, appropriately called "the second death" (20:14). The first death (which is but the shadow of death) is of the body alone; the

---

3. See, for example, J. Gwyn Griffiths, *The Divine Verdict: A Study of Divine Judgment in the Ancient Religions* (Leiden: E. J. Brill, 1991).

4. In the King James Version it occurs also at 22:19, but here all the best manuscript evidence reads "tree of life."

"second death," which is absolute unmitigated death, is final and complete separation from God, the source of life (see Matt. 10:28; Luke 12:4-5). The last verse of the chapter contains the most poignant statement of all: "Anyone whose name was not found written in the book of life was thrown into the lake of fire" (20:15).

The account in these few verses, in spite of their brevity, is one of the most impressive descriptions of the Last Judgment ever written. John's vision presents these truths better than any reasoned argument could ever do. The opening of the books suggests that our earthly lives are important and meaningful, and are taken into account at the end. But the consultation of the book of life shows that our eternal destiny is determined by God's decision, by God's grace, by God's amazing goodness.

The final judgment clears the scene for the establishment of the new heaven and the new earth, from which sin and imperfection and death are banished forevermore—as John's vision that follows reveals.

11

JOHN'S VISION OF THE HEAVENLY JERUSALEM

(Revelation 21:1–22:21)

CHAPTERS 21 and 22 provide a magnificent climax for the last book of the Bible. In the opening verses of chapter 21 John gives a short, general description of the holy city, the new Jerusalem, which he will fill out in the succeeding verses. First there is a description of the eternal blessedness of God's people in the new heaven and the new earth. Here John elaborates on the promise God had long before given to Isaiah that he would "create new heavens and a new earth" (Isa. 65:17), which would abide forever (Isa. 66:22).

Whether John would have us think of the new heavens and new earth as a transformation of the existing order, or whether this present cosmos will come to an end and a new creation will replace it, is not quite clear. In any case, the word *new* used by John does not mean simply another, but a new kind of heaven and earth. The new creation will have some continuity with creation as we now know it, yet it will be radically different. What makes it new is disclosed in the opening paragraph. Here John lays the fullest emphasis upon that without which any heaven would be but the shadow of a name—he emphasizes the presence of God. In the new order God's home will be with God's people. "He will dwell with them as their God; they will be his peoples, and God himself will be with them; he will wipe every tear from their eyes. Death will be no more; mourning and crying and pain will be no more, for the first things have passed away" (21:3-4).

Likewise in the new order, John tells us, there is to be no more sea (21:1). Behind this strange announcement lies the fact that the Jews regarded the sea as a symbol of separation and turbulence. Throughout the Bible it symbolizes restless insubordination (see Job 38:8-11; Ps. 89:9; Isa. 57:20), and in Revelation 13:1 it casts up the system that embodies hostility against God's people. Naturally, then, there is no room for it in the new creation.

The positive side of that blessedness "when the sea is no more" is pictured by a description of "the holy city, the new Jerusalem, coming down out of heaven from God, prepared as a bride adorned for her husband" (21:2). That is to say, the city originates in heaven and is beautiful beyond all comparison. The heavenly Jerusalem, John is told later (21:9-10), represents the church, and a description of that city is given in the closing vision of the book (21:9–22:5).

And now, for only the second time in the book (1:8), God speaks. Seated on the throne God declares, "See, I am making all things new" (21:5). Although these words refer primarily to the final renewing at the end, the present tense also suggests that God is continually making things new here and now (compare 2 Cor. 3:18; 4:16-18; 5:16-17; Col. 3:1-4). Again, the mighty voice of God is heard saying, "It is done!" (21:6). To the mind of the believer the consummation of all that had been predicted and promised is so certain that in a sense it may be said to have been reached before it is actually accomplished. At every stage of the struggle the believer is conscious of the final victory. Very appropriately the divine name is mentioned to underscore the completion of everything that God began: "I am the Alpha and the Omega, the beginning and the end" (21:6).

To all who are thirsty God promises to "give water as a gift from the spring of the water of life" (21:6). In lands where water is such an essential commodity, salvation is beautifully described by the symbolism of a spring and a river (22:1). The free offer of the gospel sounds clearly and repeatedly in these last two chapters.

At this point John expands his initial announcement concerning the new Jerusalem and presents an elaborate description of the heavenly city (21:9–22:5). He tells us that one of the seven angels who had the bowls of wrath spoke to him saying, "Come, I will show you the bride, the wife of the Lamb" (21:9). The angel is no doubt the one who in chapter 17 summoned John to witness the judgment of the great whore (the wicked city of Babylon). At that time John was carried away in spirit into a wilderness; now, by contrast, he is carried away in spirit to a great, high mountain so as to get, as it were, a better vision of "the holy city Jerusalem coming down out of heaven from God" (21:10).

The fact that John refers twice (21:2 and 10; see also 3:12) to the holy city as "coming down" does not mean that he saw the city come down from heaven on two separate occasions. John is identifying a permanent characteristic of the city; its nature is defined by its having come down. The expression involves more than a spatial metaphor: the city comes from God—it is not merely a voluntary association of men and women. With a sovereign disregard of rules against mixing metaphors, the beloved community (the church) is portrayed as both bride (21:9) and city (21:10-14). In the following description of the city and its magnificence, therefore, the author presents at the same time a vision of heaven in a tapestry of symbolism that describes the church triumphant in its perfected and eternal glory.

Although John's description of the city (the people of God) is meant to be symbolic, it is nevertheless pictured very precisely. The angel who was talking to John "had a measuring rod of gold to measure the city and its gates and walls" (21:15). The city measures fifteen hundred miles in length, in breadth, and in height (21:16). But how can a city be a cube? The

100

description is architecturally preposterous, and must not be taken with flat-footed literalism. In ancient times the cube was held to be the most perfect of all geometric forms. By this symbolism, therefore, John wants us to understand that the heavenly Jerusalem is absolutely splendid, with a harmony and symmetry of perfect proportions. Furthermore, he says that "the street of the city is pure gold" (21:21). In ancient times, of course, streets were not paved. In the wet season streets were mud; in dry times they were dust. What a contrast to that is the new Jerusalem, where the redeemed walk on streets of gold!

The golden city has twelve gates, each made of a huge pearl (21:21). The description is magnificently bewildering—and John intends it to be that way, so that in our imagination we may be carried along with wonder at the splendor of all that God has prepared for his people. Some individuals without much poetic sensitivity have been offended by the material grandeur ascribed to the perfect city. If they were to read with any degree of understanding the great medieval hymn, "Jerusalem the Golden,"[1] they would come to see how perfectly a poet can use material figures to express spiritual meaning.

---

1. Two stanzas of the hymn, translated by John Mason Neale (1851) from Bernard of Cluny's lengthy poem, "De Contemptu Mundi," may serve as a sample.

> Jerusalem the golden,
> With milk and honey blest!
> Beneath thy contemplation
> Sink heart and voice oppressed.
> I know not, O I know not
> What joys await us there;
> What radiancy of glory,
> What bliss beyond compare.

> O sweet and blessed country,
> The home of God's elect!
> O sweet and blessed country
> That eager hearts expect!
> Jesu, in mercy bring us
> To that dear land of rest:
> Who art, with God the Father
> And Spirit, ever blest.

Bernard's poem, "On contempt of the World," running to about three thousand lines, was really written as a bitter satire on the corruptions current in the twelfth century at Cluny when he was an occupant at the monastery. Within its walls were jealousy, scandal, and strife. After castigating these expressions of worldliness, Bernard then turns his thought, wistfully and longingly, to a realm where such evils will be banished, and pure worship and true love will order all.

John next turns his attention to aspects of life within this incredible city. The reader is no doubt surprised that he presents heaven without a temple. Unlike Ezekiel, who spends four chapters (40–43) in a detailed description of the new temple, John says, "I saw no temple in the city" (21:22). There is no temple or sanctuary in the holy city, for, in one respect, the city itself is all sanctuary. Its dimensions, being in the form of a cube, are like the Holy of Holies in the Mosaic tabernacle of old. The immediate presence of God is no longer in a reserved place, entered only by the high priest, and that but once a year; God is now accessible to all. The assurance that the city's "gates will never be shut by day" (21:25) conveys the sense of perfect freedom of access and fellowship with God. Normally the gates of ancient cities were closed during the night for security reasons, but the gates of this city do not need to be closed, for "there will be no night there" (21:25).

The angel shows John a sparkling river that flows crystal-clear from the heavenly throne, which indicates its boundless supply (22:1). It was the hope of Israelite prophets that living waters would flow from Jerusalem in the age to come (Ezek. 47:1-12; Zech. 14:8), and the psalmist spoke of a "river whose streams make glad the city of God" (Ps. 46:4). Reminiscent of the garden of Eden (Gen. 2:9), the tree[2] of life is present here, standing on either side of the river and yielding twelve kinds of fruit. Besides producing fruit to be eaten, the tree also has leaves that "are for the healing of the nations" (22:2). The saving benefits of the gospel promote the well-being of all aspects of personal and communal life.

Another link with the account in the opening chapters of Genesis is John's declaration that in the holy city there will no longer be anything accursed (22:3). After Adam and Eve had sinned by eating of the tree of knowledge, they were banished from Eden by the mercy of God lest they eat also of the tree of life and become immortal in their sin (Gen. 3:22-24). Now

---

2. Here the term *tree*, though singular in number, bears a collective sense.

that redemption has been accomplished, it is safe to eat from the tree of life. Paradise lost is now paradise regained.

At this point the seer of Patmos directs the reader's attention to the most important feature of all: namely, that the throne of God and of the Lamb will be in the heavenly Jerusalem, and that God's servants "will worship him; they will see his face, and his name will be on their foreheads" (22:3-4). Then the promise in Jesus' beatitude will be realized, namely, that "the pure in heart . . . will see God" (Matt. 5:8). But what does it mean to see God? St. Augustine wrestled with this question in his classic work, *The City of God*.[3] He asks whether, in heaven, when we close our eyelids, we will shut out the beatific vision. Very sensibly he concludes that this cannot be true, for to see God means more than to look at God, to gaze at God. In heaven, he says, "God will be seen by the eyes of the heart, which can see realities that are immaterial." Here Augustine is reminding us that the verb to see also means to comprehend and understand. In its totality, then, one can say that to see God involves being near God, knowing God, and rejoicing in God all at the same time.

John's words, however, go beyond the thought of seeing God by either sensory or spiritual perception; he says that God's servants "will see his face" (22:4). What special nuance of meaning does this expression convey? In antiquity to see the face of the king signified more than simply glancing up at the king when he might be riding by. The expression implied that one was granted an audience with the king, and an opportunity to present one's petition in direct personal conversation (Gen. 43:3, 5; Exod. 10:28, 29; and elsewhere). Thus, to see God's face is not only to be in God's nearer presence, but also to enjoy a relationship of absolute trust and openness. This is confirmed by John's following assertion, that God's "name will be on their foreheads," signifying their preciousness to God to whom they belong. In short, John is telling his

---

3. Book XXII, chapter 29.

readers that one day there will be granted to the servants of God that which had previously been the privilege of the heavenly creatures around God's throne (4:2-11; see also Matt. 18:10).

There is an old saying that in heaven everyone's cup of joy will be full, but some cups will be larger than others. That is, the degree to which we shall be able to see God will depend in part on the perfecting of our spiritual vision here and now. This is why the Bible exhorts Christians to "grow in the grace and knowledge of our Lord and Savior Jesus Christ" (2 Pet. 3:18). As we make progress in the Christian life we gain greater capacity to know and understand God. "Now we see in a mirror, dimly, but then we will see face to face" (1 Cor. 13:12; 1 John 3:1-3).

The combination of purity with the vision of God is made not only in the Sermon on the Mount (Matt. 5:8, quoted above) but is also reiterated more than once by early Christian writers. The author of the Letter to the Hebrews exhorts his readers to "pursue . . . holiness without which no one will see God" (Heb. 12:14). Though Christian believers are described as children of God, they are not yet what they will be hereafter, for when the Lord appears, "we will be like him, for we will see him as he is. And all who have this hope in him purify themselves, just as he is pure" (1 John 3:2).

EPILOGUE: CLOSING WARNINGS AND PROMISES

At first reading the concluding verses of Revelation appear to be a discordant assortment of brief, staccato-like warnings and promises. But more careful attention discloses the work of an artist who skillfully reiterates features that were introduced in the opening section of his book. Besides affirming the authenticity of his visionary experiences (22:6 and 1:10-11), he characterizes his book as a genuine prophecy (22:7 and 1:3), and indicates that it is to be read aloud in churches (22:18 and 1:3). John claims for his work a threefold authentication: namely, God (22:6 and 1:1), Christ (22:16 and 1:1), and the angels who mediated it (22:16 and 1:1).

In sharp contrast to Daniel, who was told to seal up the record of his visions "until the time of the end" (Dan. 12:4, 9), John is commanded, "Do not seal up the words of the prophecy of this book, for the time is near" (22:10). In fact, the concluding verses reiterate four times (verses 6, 7, 12, 20) a theme found only three times in the rest of the book (1:1; 2:16; 3:11), namely, that Christ will come soon and that the interval before his return will be short. Because the time is short, there will be but little opportunity for repentance and change: the wicked are confirmed in their wickedness, the righteous in their righteousness (22:11; compare Dan. 12:10).

In the Christian doctrine of the last things, the imminence of the end is moral rather than chronological; each successive generation, so far as can be known to the contrary, may be the last generation. In that sense the time is always near (22:10). It is therefore the part of wisdom for believers to be ready to meet their Lord.

The last two of the seven beatitudes in Revelation pronounce a blessing upon those who obey the prophetic message contained in the book (22:7), and upon those who wash (present tense) their robes (22:14). The washing of one's robes is in 7:14 connected with the sacrifice of Christ; it is not a matter of self-reformation but the saving and purifying effect of identifying with Jesus' death. It is these who "will have the right to the tree of life and may enter the city by the gates" (22:14). The privilege of entrance is heightened by listing those who are excluded: "Outside are the dogs and sorcerers and fornicators and murderers and idolaters, and everyone who loves and practices falsehood" (22:15). "Outside" does not mean that they are in close proximity to the city; for the idea of "outside" we should compare Jesus' reference to "the outer darkness" (Matt. 8:12). This list of those who are excluded resembles in some respects the earlier list of those consigned to the lake of fire (21:8), but here the first category

105

is "the dogs"—a reference to sodomites. The sentence in the original is abrupt, as expressing abhorrence.

When books were copied by hand, scribes would occasionally add comments of their own or leave out words they thought were unsuitable. John therefore includes at the end of his book a solemn warning (similar to that found in Deut. 4:2; 12:32) declaring that nothing should be added or deleted, for the very good reason that it is a revelation from God (22:18-19). We might see this as the ancient equivalent of copyright.

* * * * * * * *

The book of Revelation provided pastoral encouragement for Christians who were confronted with persecution and cruelty. The book was written, we know, to enable them to control their fear, to renew their commitment, and to sustain their vision. John's final sentence is a benediction: " The grace of the Lord Jesus be with all the saints" (22:21). Thus, the concluding note is one of comfort, of love, of encouragement. There could be no more fitting end for a book that contains horrible visions of great monsters and catastrophic judgments. John closes his book with visions of hope and of heaven, promising that at the last we shall enjoy the vision of God because of the grace of the Lord Jesus Christ.

FOR FURTHER READING

In addition to consulting articles in Bible dictionaries concerning John, Patmos, Ephesus, Smyrna, Antipas, Nicolaitans, and other names that occur in the book of Revelation, the following will be of assistance in further study.

Aune, David E. *Word Biblical Commentary.* vol. 52A. *Revelation 1–5.* Dallas: Word, 1997 (ccxi + 374 pages); vol. 52B. *Revelation 6–16.* Nashville: Thomas Nelson Publishers, 1998 (xlv + 375-903 pages); and vol. 52C. *Revelation 17–22.* Nashville: Thomas Nelson Publishers, 1998 (xlvi + 904-1354 pages).

Barclay, William. *The Revelation of John.* 2 vols. Philadelphia: Westminster Press, 1959. A useful commentary, designed primarily for laypeople (231 and 297 pages).

Boring, M. Eugene. *Revelation.* Louisville: John Knox Press, 1989. A volume in the series Interpretation, A Bible Commentary for Teaching and Preaching (236 pages).

Caird, George B. *The Revelation of St. John the Divine.* New York: Harper & Row, 1968. A standard, verse-by-verse commentary (318 pages).

Ewert, David. *The Church Under Fire.* Hillsboro, Kans.: Kindred Press, 1988. A helpful and balanced exposition, with present-day applications (175 pages).

Kealy, Seán P., C.S.Sp. *The Apocalypse of John.* Wilmington, Del.: Michael Glazier, 1989. This is volume 15 in the series Message of Biblical Spirituality (260 pages).

Mounce, Robert H. *The Book of Revelation.* Grand Rapids: Wm. B. Eerdmans, 1977. A detailed, scholarly work in the series New International Commentary on the New Testament (426 pages).

Rowland, Christopher C. "The Book of Revelation: Introduction, Commentary, and Reflections," vol. XII *The New Interpreter's Bible.* Nashville: Abingdon Press, 1998 (501-748 pages).

Schüssler Fiorenza, Elisabeth. *Revelation: Vision of a Just World.* Minneapolis: Fortress Press, 1991. Assessment of Revelation in terms of liberation and feminist theology (150 pages).

Stott, John R. W. *What Christ Thinks of the Church.* Grand Rapids: Wm. B. Eerdmans, 1958. This book deals with chapters 1 to 3 of Revelation (128 pages).

Sweet, J. P. M. *Revelation.* Philadelphia: Westminster Press, 1979. A detailed commentary on all passages of the book of Revelation (361 pages).

Wall, Robert W. *Revelation.* Peabody, Mass.: Hendrickson Publishers, 1991. A volume in the series New International Biblical Commentary (295 pages).

For discussion of the millennium and chapter 20 of Revelation, see the books mentioned in footnote 2 on page 95 above.

SUBJECT INDEX

LEADER'S GUIDE
Donn Downall

CONTENTS

Ideas for Bible Study

Using Videotape

Many adults have become familiar with the videocassette recorder (VCR) in recent years. In a typical class several persons may be familiar with the equipment and willing to operate it for the class.

The use of videotape provides a way to encounter capable Christian scholars who can bring the Bible to life in rewarding ways.

However, using video for Bible study is different from using video for entertainment. An encounter with the Word of God is taking place. Each person in the viewing group is involved not only in one-way communication from the screen, but also in interactive communication with the Scripture. For that reason the participation time before and after each recorded presentation is a vital part of each session. Dick Murray, a well-known Christian educator, in *Teaching the Bible to Adults and Youth* (Abingdon Press, 1987; pages 82-83), has pointed out the following advantages and disadvantages in using a Bible scholar on videotape:

Strengths of Using a Bible Scholar

A videotaped presentation by a Bible scholar offers us the following:
1. A rich store of information gained from years of study.
2. A personal commitment to a lifelong pursuit of understanding the background and complexities of the Scripture.
3. A trained and disciplined imagination, which can often discern connections and implications not available to the average person.
4. An animated and often contagious excitement for the subject, which can be very stimulating to those who hear.

Limitations of Using a Bible Scholar

1. It is easy for most of us to allow scholars to do all the work with the Scripture, while we sit back and think, *Wow! That is very interesting!*
2. Once the scholar has spoken, it is very difficult for many to advance a contrary opinion of their own, even when there is real room for disagreement.
3. The scholar is always speaking from a particular perspective, and often does not acknowledge any possibility of a contrary opinion.

Studying Revelation

In the laundromat, on TV or radio talk shows, and elsewhere you may hear persons talking about the Book of Revelation. They speculate on its mysterious relation to the future of humankind. Their theories are expounded with passion, but how many of them have carefully examined the Book of Revelation itself? Essential to this study are the insights presented by Dr. Bruce M. Metzger in his book, *Breaking the Code: Understanding the Book of Revelation* and in his lessons on the videotape. Even more essential will be each participant's own Bible. (Dr. Metzger usually reads from the **New Revised Standard Version**, but any version or a variety of versions will be useful in the class.) Personal encounters between the class member and the Bible will reveal a wide variety of literary forms used by the author of the Book of Revelation. Dr. Metzger doesn't stop at every chapter and verse. The passages for class members to examine each week are samples from the portions Dr. Metzger uses in his book and in his video presentations.

Throughout the study the class will need the opportunity to return to a key question:

What message do you find in this passage for you or for your congregation?

You may wish to print that question on posterboard so that it will be available for each lesson.

LESSON ONE

PURPOSE

To appreciate and understand the Book of Revelation as a carefully written document that used symbolism and code language to reinforce for Christians long ago a commitment to be faithful in spite of the brutal oppression they were enduring.

SUGGESTED PROCEDURE

If class members are not acquainted with one another, have them introduce themselves and respond briefly to a question such as, "When you were a young child, first grade or younger, what puzzled you or frightened you about the Bible?" Suggest that class members take notes during Dr. Metzger's video presentations, or write in the margins of the book as they read. Learners need ways to retain their own points of interest and questions to ponder. Remind them of an Asian proverb, "The faintest ink is more lasting than the strongest memory."

Ask learners to open their Bibles to the first chapter of Revelation. Use a reader or readers to present aloud four segments of that chapter. Mention that the readings differ somewhat from the sequence in which they appear in the Bible:

Revelation 1:9-11
Revelation 1:4-8
Revelation 1:10-20 (repeating verses 10 and 11 from first reading)
Revelation 1:1-3

Call attention to "the one who reads aloud" and "those who hear"(verse 3). Ask someone to find in *Breaking the Code*, page 22, several reasons why reading aloud was specifically mentioned.

Draw a horizontal line on chalkboard or newsprint. (If none is available, stand with your arms outstretched.) Point out the two "far ends." Mention that some Christians are at one end, avoiding the Book of Revelation as much as they can. At the other extreme are those who are so enamored by the Book of Revelation that they pay more attention to it than to the Sermon on the Mount, the Book of Psalms, or other key portions of Scripture.

Ask if any members of the group believe themselves to be at one extreme or the other. Invite them to explain why they think so.

At this point allow 17 minutes to watch
Video Lesson One if it is available.

In Dr. Metzger's book, on pages 17-18, he writes about the "literary genre" of Revelation. Ask someone to find what he calls the two basic features of most apocalypses.

Remind the group that Dr. Metzger offered three presuppositions to help persons understand this unique book of Scripture. Invite class members to try to recall these presuppositions:

1. We should take seriously what the author says; for example, when John said he had a vision, we need to accept it as a vision.
2. John used the language of symbolism to describe his visions; therefore, John's word-pictures need to be understood as symbolic representations of the divine Word received by John.
3. We should not assume that the sequence in which John received or wrote the visions has to be the order in which the content of the visions must be fulfilled; evidence seems to suggest that John sometimes stopped to review or to repeat an earlier thought.

The third presupposition leads to a frequently raised question:

Is the Book of Revelation a calendar or timeline that reveals the future?

Two statements about Jesus Christ may influence the way we answer that question:

1. Jesus Christ will return to earth after certain events happen.
2. Jesus Christ is with God's people now. (See Matthew 18:20.)

Remind the group members that it is possible for both these statements to be true. Individuals, however, may think one statement is more important than the other. Ask for a show of hands to indicate which statement group members consider more important.

Review Dr. Metzger's remarks about Revelation 1:20, "the seven lampstands are the seven churches." Why does he remind us that in

Revelation 1:13 we find Christ "in the midst of the lampstands"? Encourage comments or questions by class members.

If time is available, seek from class members responses to this key question, which will be included in some form in each lesson:

What message do you find in this passage for you or for your congregation?

You may also wish to consider this additional discussion topic if there is time:

Notice the wording of Revelation 1:9. How is it possible to share "persecution" and "the kingdom" at the same time?

POINTERS FOR LEADERS: THE APOCALYPTIC GENRE

Class members may not be familiar with the term *genre*, (ZHON-ruh), a French word referring to a particular type or category of literature. On page 17 Dr. Metzger mentions several other writings in the apocalyptic genre, and identifies two common features of all such writings. Political realities often made code language necessary to keep oppressors from understanding the writing if it should fall into their hands. For instance, the woman called "Babylon" is a code word for Rome, a city built on seven hills. (See Revelation 17:9.)

Close by asking someone (who has agreed in advance) to offer a prayer, or use the following prayer:

> **God, we seek to understand you better through your Word. Today we have begun to think about some puzzling words. Help us appreciate one another as you appreciate us. When we question ideas and disagree with one another or with the lecturer, remind us that we are sometimes wrong. You know when we are wrong. We admit that we are often wrong, even though we never can say, "At this moment I am wrong." Forgive us, keep us humble, and because of your love for us help us grow in our love for your Word, for one another, and for your Son Jesus Christ.**

LESSON TWO

PURPOSE

To become acquainted with the Book of Revelation's seven messages to seven churches and find in them meaning for congregations today.

SUGGESTED PROCEDURE

Begin today by calling attention to the messages to seven churches in Revelation 2 and 3. Assign each class member **one** of the seven. Have them locate and read aloud the part of their message that comes after each of these phrases (each is repeated seven times):

> These are the words of . . .
> I know . . .
> Let anyone who has an ear . . .

This activity ought to call attention to the careful literary work that is found in the Book of Revelation. The planned repetition, seven varied and imaginative descriptions of the heavenly Christ, and the precise identifications of each church's strengths and weaknesses are all indications of the talent of the author.

Turn to Dr. Metzger's book, pages 29-30 for further discussion of the literary structure of the seven messages to the churches.

Allow 14 minutes at this point to watch Video Lesson Two if it is available. Check with participants from last week to see if the sound volume, the seating, or the lighting was right. Total darkness is not necessary for watching a video.

Assign each of the seven messages in Revelation 2 and 3 to at least one person. (Two of the messages could be combined for a smaller group.) Ask that the messages be read silently, then that the readers respond to the key question:

What message do you find in this passage for you or for your congregation?

If time permits, consider this additional discussion question:

In Revelation 2 and 3 who are the conquerors?

Discuss any leftover questions from last week as well as the class members' responses today.

Remind the group that on the video Dr. Metzger quotes the Scottish Bible scholar, William Barclay: "A lukewarm Christian has no claim to be a Christian at all."

Draw a rough version of a Fahrenheit thermometer, showing the boiling point, 212 degrees; freezing point, 32 degrees; and three or four numbers in between, such as 50, 100, and 150. Invite each class member mentally to place himself or herself on the scale.

POINTERS FOR LEADERS:
THE BRANCH DAVIDIAN TRAGEDY

On the videotape Dr. Metzger says, "The presence of Christ departs when well-intentioned people, zealous to find the right way, depart from the ultimate way which is love." You may wish to relate his words to the tragedy at the Branch Davidian compound.

Ask if any or all of the Branch Davidians were well-intentioned. Were they zealous? Had they departed from "the ultimate way which is love"? At what point? What was their reason for stockpiling vast quantities of weapons and ammunition? Viewers may want to talk about this unfortunate example of human destruction. If so, remind them that the message to the church at Ephesus includes these words: "You have tested those who claim to be apostles, but are not, and have found them to be false" (Revelation 2:2). Ask how many in your group think of the Branch Davidians as false apostles, and how many do not. Invite class members to explain their positions.

POINTERS FOR LEADERS:
CHURCHES IN SEVEN CITIES

Class members may be interested in what is known about the seven churches other than what is found in the Book of Revelation. Only three are mentioned elsewhere in the New Testament. Ephesus is the best known, receiving major attention in Acts 18—20, and in several of Paul's letters (including, of course, the Letter to the Ephesians).

An important woman in the early church, Lydia, is usually associated with Philippi, where Paul met her. Acts 16:14 tells us she was originally from Thyatira.

A bit of mystery surrounds the church at Laodicea. It is mentioned several times by Paul in his Letter to the Colossians. He said he sent a letter to Laodicea. He wanted the two letters to be exchanged so that both congregations would hear both letters (Colossians 4:16).

Was Paul's letter to the Laodiceans been lost? When he wrote to Philemon, he addressed the letter to a man named Archippus, as well. Archippus is to be given a special message by the Colossians (4:17). Also, near the end of both letters, Philemon and Colossians, Paul named the same five companions, who joined him in sending greetings.

The other four churches that received messages in Revelation are mentioned nowhere else in the New Testament.

To bring the lesson to a close offer the following prayer or similar thoughts:

> **Lord, you can see our hidden selves and hear our unspoken thoughts, you know the temperature of our faith, when we are frozen Christians and when we are steaming with desire to serve our Savior. Kindle through the Scriptures the fire that can warm our hearts, we pray in Jesus' name.**

LESSON THREE

PURPOSE

To recognize and appreciate how symbolism helps us grasp abstract concepts, such as our idea of heaven, and to consider the role of Christ in God's eternal plan for humans who seek to be faithful and obedient to their Lord.

SUGGESTED PROCEDURE

Ask the group members to find Revelation 4 in their Bibles. Ask one-third of the group to read aloud the first sentence (ending with "a door stood open"). Ask another third to read aloud the next sentence (ending with "what must take place after this"). Ask the last third to read verse 2 that ends with the words "one seated on the throne" (verse 2).

Invite each class member to try to picture, in his or her mind's eye, what the "one" looked like. (Note, when ready, that the one is not described as having the form or shape of any creature, human or animal, large or small, male or female. Instead, this one seems to resemble colored lights or shining jewels.) Ask the group members to let their mind's eye again picture the words of the Scripture.

Read 4:3-11 aloud. Then ask everyone to read together the song in verse 11. Point out that the song makes clear that the one on the throne is God.

Then ask the group to turn to 5:9 and read aloud another song that begins with the same words, "You are worthy." Go back to the beginning of Revelation 5. Point out that God holds a scroll fastened with seven seals, and that no one is found who can open the seals until the coming of a lion is announced (the Lion of the tribe of Judah). But instead comes a Lamb. Ask, "Who is the Lamb?" (The answer: Jesus Christ.)

At this point in today's lesson ask each member of the class to talk to one other person about the key question:

What message do you find in this passage for you or for your congregation?

The pairs of learners will not need to report to the total class unless they desire to do so.

At this point take 17 minutes to watch
Video Lesson Three if it is available.

Ask class members if they remember what Dr. Metzger referred to as a change of location between Revelation 3 and Revelation 4.

In the second paragraph of chapter 5 in *Breaking the Code* (page 47), the meaning of the words, "Come up here," is explained. (Revelation 2 and 3 were focused on this earth, specifically on seven communities, and the church in each of them. In Revelation 4 and 5 the focus changes to heaven.)

Jot down on the chalkboard or on paper brief descriptions of how class members would describe heaven. ("Streets of gold," "many mansions," "beyond the sunset," are some possible phrases.)

Suggest that each person look in the Bible to see how John describes heaven in Revelation 4:2-7. What is mentioned first? What does the central place of the throne suggest about God? Are class members comfortable with the idea of God sitting on a throne?

Ask the group to mention other images of God that the Bible gives us. (shepherd, rock, and so forth) Ask if it makes a difference how God is described when we think of God welcoming us to heaven. Encourage the class members to talk of what they picture heaven to be.

If time permits, consider these additional discussion questions:

What do the songs, such as Revelation 4:8-11 and 5:9-14, suggest about the kind of singing done in the early church? How can Christ be the Lion of the tribe of Judah and the slaughtered Lamb at the same time? (See Revelation 5:5-6.)

Dismiss the group with this prayer:

O God our help and our eternal home, we thank you for the words of our Bible that help us keep our imaginations working. The man of Patmos described you as Holy, Holy, Holy. We know that you are three times better than the best we can imagine. As we continue to study your Revelation to John, let his astonishing words enter freely into our minds that we may stretch our wonder and our praise, through Jesus Christ the Lamb of God.

LESSON FOUR

Breaking the Code, chapter 6; Revelation 6:1—8:4

PURPOSE

To increase our understanding of the style and function of apocalyptic literature and begin to clarify how God's gift of free will allows human beings either creative faithfulness, which brings God's rewards, or sinful usurpation of divine power, which brings God's judgment.

SUGGESTED PROCEDURE

Select four readers to read aloud the following verses from Revelation 6 as group members follow in their Bibles:

6:1-2

6:3-4

6:5-6

6:7-8

When the readers have finished, ask how many class members have heard of this particular vision before. What have they understood it to mean? Take a few minutes to discuss the key question:

What message do you find in this passage for you or for your congregation?

Make note of points for further discussion after the taped presentation by Dr. Metzger.

At this time turn on Video Lesson Four if you have it available. The time required is 16 minutes.

Ask three readers each to find in their Bibles one of the following passages:

Revelation 4:6-8

Ezekiel 1:4-14

Isaiah 6:1-8

On the chalkboard write the headings for three columns:

LIVING CREATURES   HORSE   RIDER

Ask class members to listen to the three readings, then be ready to help complete a chart based on Revelation 6:1-8. Explain that we find similar references (to "living creatures" or "seraphs") in each of these books of the Bible. Compare what these accounts tell us about the appearance and the roles of the "living creatures." (They sing God's praises, attend to God's wishes, and guard and use God's purifying fire.)

Ask a class member to read the verses about the first horse and rider (6:1-2) as you write on the chart:

LIVING CREATURES	HORSE	RIDER
1. voice of thunder; calls "Come!"	white	bow and crown conquest

Continue to fill in the chart for the other three:

2. Come!	red	sword; slaughter
3. Come!	black	scales; economic depression
4. Come!	pale green (color of decaying flesh)	named Death; sword; famine; pestilence; wild animals

Discuss insights and questions about this vision of the four horsemen. Ask if class members think that their importance in the Book of Revelation may have been exaggerated by readers in recent centuries. Consider if the four living creatures, whose roles are positive, not destructive, may offer more meaning for our faith.

Turn to page 51 in *Breaking the Code* and identify what Dr. Metzger describes as the function of the four living creatures.

Discuss class members' ideas about what causes conquest, bloodshed, inflation, and other social evils. Then mention these words of Dr. Metzger from the tape, "God does not approve of famine and death and hell, **but** . . ."

Ask, "But what?" Then repeat the entire sentence as Dr. Metzger stated it: "God does not approve of famine and death and hell, but they are what must follow if people persist in opposing God's rule."

Remind the group that Dr. Metzger compares what happens when we ignore a physical law and step off a cliff with the disasterous consequences of ignoring God's moral laws.

Discuss what Dr. Metzger has to say on page 57 of his book about power and free will.

If time permits, consider these additional discussion questions:

What images are used in Revelation 7:15-17 to describe the bliss of the redeemed in glory? Do they have any special meaning for persecuted believers?

POINTERS FOR LEADERS:
ARTISTS, WRITERS, AND REVELATION

The videotapes for *Breaking the Code* make use of brief glimpses of artists' interpretations of scenes described in Revelation. Each painting or sketch is the work of a particular artist from a particular cultural background and a particular time in history. They serve in the videos to provide changes of visual foreground, and are not meant to suggest "correct" imagery to match the words of John of Patmos as Dr. Metzger interprets them. A list of the art and photographs used in the video appears on page 31 of this guide.

If class members have a special interest in art that relates to the Book of Revelation, you may wish to consult a high school or college teacher of art. Such a person could give you ideas to help explain how art masterpieces relate to various parts of the Bible, especially the imaginative apocalyptic sections. You may wish to invite the art instructor to visit a session of your group.

Two books listed on page 29 of this guide emphasize Revelation's influence on the fine arts. *Mysterious Apocalypse* by Arthur Wainwright is worth examining for its art. If class members are interested in drawing connections between apocalyptic parts of the Bible and contemporary literature, you may suggest consulting selected entries in *A Dictionary of Biblical Tradition in English Literature,* edited by D.L. Jeffrey.

As a prayer to close the session you may wish to use these words:

> **Too often, O God of righteousness, we have limited our tears and anger to pain that has touched us or may touch us in the future. Forgive us. Remind us that your love for your creation is "like the wideness of the sea." Help us be faithful to you, and make us confident that you are Lord of all the universe and of all that will face your children throughout this life and throughout the vastness of eternity. We pray through him who continues to give us glimpses of his victory, Jesus Christ our Lord.**

LESSON FIVE

Breaking the Code, chapter 7; Revelation 8:5—11:19

PURPOSE

To realize through the vivid and horrible symbolism of the Book of Revelation that divine judgment does not mean that God desires to inflict vengeance, rather that God wills to bring people to repentance.

SUGGESTED PROCEDURE

Begin this session by asking if anyone has ever been in a swarm of locusts. If so, allow time for a brief description of what it was like. Ask class members to close their Bibles except for someone who will read aloud 9:3 through 9:10. With Bibles still closed, see how much the group can remember of the description of the locusts. After a few moments, have them open their Bibles and check their memories against the actual text.

A devastating natural disaster such as swarming locusts could have been experienced by John and at least some of his readers. Their familiarity with disasters probably made the descriptive language of Revelation even more vivid.

Invite the learners to check page 64 of *Breaking the Code* to be reminded of a major catastrophe that hit the Roman world in A.D. 79. Ask how the memories or reports of that event might have influenced John's "disciplined imagination."

Dr. Metzger has so far taken us through eleven of the twenty-two chapters in the Book of Revelation. At this halfway point a review of certain features will be valuable. If class members each have a Bible, they will be able to see the progression in the outline that follows. If not, use your Bible and the chalkboard.

Seven in Revelation 1—4 - messages to churches
Seven in Revelation 5:1-4 - seals that can be opened by no one but
    the Lamb:
Revelation 6:1 - first seal, first horse and rider
Revelation 6:3 - second seal, second horse and rider
Revelation 6:5 - third seal, third horse and rider

Revelation 6:7 - fourth seal, fourth horse and rider
Revelation 6:9 - fifth seal, martyrs sheltered beneath altar
Revelation 6:12-17 - sixth seal, great earthquake
Revelation 8:1 - seventh seal, a half-hour of silence in heaven

At this point mention that Dr. Metzger in today's presentation says that the next series of sevens comes in rapid-fire order: seven angels blowing seven trumpets.

You might mention that the use of "seven" in John's writing is not always obvious. Dr. Metzger points out (*Breaking the Code,* page 22) seven "beatitudes." (See page 30 of this guide.)

If you have Video Lesson Five available, allow
15 minutes to show it now. Suggest that the group
be alert for an answer to this question: "To what Old Testament events
does Dr. Metzger compare the plagues visited on God's enemies when
the trumpet sounds?"
(The plagues that Pharaoh and the land of Egypt suffered because they
kept God's people in slavery.)

Turn again to the key question:

What message do you find in this passage for you or for your congregation?

If time permits, consider this additional discussion question:

As you recall the locusts described in Revelation 9:3-10, can you think of some demonic "locusts" that afflict society today?

Close with an appropriate prayer, containing ideas such as the following:

> **God almighty and all-powerful, throughout your Word and throughout history we see your power overcoming your enemies. They can do great harm, but cannot avoid your verdict and your vengeance. How grateful we are that, though at times we have turned against you and lived in defiance of your will, yet your great mercy invites us back to your forgiveness and your friendship. Forgive now whatever we confess to you in silence, and restore us with your steadfast love to the company of your people.**

LESSON SIX

Breaking the Code, chapter 8; Revelation 12:1—14:20

PURPOSE

To see that beyond the symbolism and code language of the Book of Revelation, God's righteousness and love require the possibility of eternal condemnation because God respects our free will and never forces us to repent.

SUGGESTED PROCEDURE

Write on chalkboard or poster board the following questions:

How is the woman described?
What is expected of the son she bears?
Who wants to destroy the child?
Where is the child taken for safety?

Ask half the group to read silently Matthew 2:1-21. Ask the others to read silently Revelation 12:1-9. Ask each group to report how the passage they read answers the above questions. Without implying that the author of Revelation has deliberately used Matthew's account of Jesus' birth as a pattern, compare the answers.

Ask the group to turn to *Breaking the Code*, page 72. Notice what Dr. Metzger has to say about the relationship between these two radically different passages of Scripture.

If you are using the video lessons, at this time allow
17 minutes to watch Video Lesson Six.

Ask members of the class to think about how many numbers that they need for identification in our society. Some will be able to tell their auto license number, Social Security number, phone number, nine-digit zip code, and perhaps others. Offer to give them an additional personal number, a number representing their name.

Use the chalkboard or newsprint to explain that the letters of the Greek alphabet, in sets of ten, also served as numerals. Tell the class that if each letter of the English alphabet had an equivalent number the pattern might be something like this:

A = 1	J = 10	S = 100
B = 2	K = 20	T = 200
C = 3	L = 30	U = 300
D = 4	M = 40	V = 400
E = 5	N = 50	W = 500
F = 6	O = 60	X = 600
G = 7	P = 70	Y = 700
H = 8	Q = 80	Z = 800
I = 9	R = 90	

Make clear to the class that the list is an approximation only; in English there are no equivalents between our alphabet and our numerical system. Spell a few names of class members and add the numbers represented by each letter to illustrate the idea. Use the names William and Marcia for examples:

W = 500		
I = 9	M =	40
L = 30	A =	1
L = 30	R =	90
I = 9	C =	3
A = 1	I =	9
M = 40	A =	1
619		144

Learners may enjoy and remember the activity if they try to determine a number for their own name or the name of some famous person now living.

Ask class members what they have heard about the number 666. Many persons seem to believe that number to be a mystery central to the Book of Revelation. Ask if anyone can suggest a reason why 666 would be so important. Why hasn't equal importance been given to dozens of other symbols in Revelation? Ask the group to name some of the other symbols used by John, such as the lampstands that are the seven churches or the vision of the New Jerusalem.

To see 666 as a numerical representation of a name (possibly Nero Caesar or "Neron" Caesar) takes away some of the mystery. Remembering how the writer of the Book of Revelation has used numbers elsewhere, consider 144,000. In Revelation 7:5-8 we see that a thousand, a number suggesting completeness, is multiplied by 12, the number of the tribes of Israel, and again by 12. Twelve is also the number of Jesus' apostles. Ask, "Will God's redeemed sons and daughters be counted so that after 143,999 only one more will be accepted, and everyone else excluded?" Remind the group that most often in the Book of Revelation numbers are symbols, not to be taken literally.

Apply the key question to today's lesson.

What message do you find in this part of the Book of Revelation for you or for your congregation?

Close the lesson with a prayer such as:

> **God of grace and God of judgment, we are a part of humankind. Our actions as individuals have too often failed to recognize or stand against corporate and global wrongs. The power of evil has overwhelmed our feeble calls for charity and justice. But you, O God, are greater than the forces that oppose you. Help us know how to trust you, to be faithful to your purposes, and to wait for your time of judgment.**

LESSON SEVEN

PURPOSE

To see in the increasingly intense calamity and terror of the Book of Revelation the need for God's faithful servants to be prepared for long and bitter suffering without allowing discouragement or doubt to destroy their faith.

SUGGESTED PROCEDURE

Write on the chalkboard the five Bible references that follow. Assign to each member of the group one or more of these passages, all of which are songs:

Revelation 5:13-14; 7:11-12; 11:16; 12:10-12; 15:3-4.

Ask group members to read aloud these songs. Point out that the tense dramatic action of John's visions is periodically relieved by these songs of praise. This great poetry has often influenced anthems and musical works such as Handel's *Messiah*.

Write the word *Babylon* on the chalkboard or on a sheet of paper taped where all class members can see it. Ask, "What did this word probably mean to the original readers of Revelation?"

At this point use 16 minutes to show Video Lesson Seven.

When the tape is finished, ask everyone to turn in their Bibles to chapter 18 of Revelation. Suggest that learners look for similar words in verses 10, 16, and 19 ("Alas, alas, the great city"). Call attention to the name of the city, Babylon, found in verses 2, 10, and 21. Babylon, whose military power had conquered Judah six centuries earlier, had long ago passed into history for the original readers of the Book of Revelation. Suggest to your group members that "Babylon" in Revelation is probably a code word (for Rome).

Ask class members to find page 88 in *Breaking the Code*. Ask what Dr. Metzger sees in the term *Babylon* as allegorical for today. (ways that nations create idols: material abundance; military prowess; technological sophistication; imperial grandeur; and racial pride)

In each case national accomplishments are falsely considered greater than the One who created the nations. Ask for examples of each of the five, either from past history or from the present time.

Direct the discussion from forms of national idolatry to another statement near the end of the video lesson: "To the extent that ecclesiastical denominations have also succumbed to the lure of power and prestige, the words of John are applicable also to present-day church structures."

Ask how many agree that religious organizations sometimes elevate their bureaucracies, traditions, and leaders so that creatures come before the Creator. Discuss how the church could avoid receiving the wrath of God. (Possible answers might include giving more importance to the Bible, to repentence, or to reformation.)

POINTERS FOR LEADERS: REVELATION IN SONG

Some of the best-loved music of the church is based on parts of the Book of Revelation. You may wish to sing, to listen to, and/or to examine the texts of some of these:

"The Battle Hymn of the Republic," by Julia Ward Howe (Revelation 14:17-20)

"Holy, Holy, Holy," by Reginald Heber (Revelation 4)

"The Holy City," by Adolphe Adam (Revelation 21 and 22)

"The Hallelujah Chorus" from *Messiah,* by George Frederick Handel (Revelation 11:15; 19;1,7)

Close the lesson with prayer, perhaps using these words:

O God whom we worship when two or three or thousands gather in the name of Christ, we thank you for the church, which in spite of human pride and selfishness shows us a path to follow. Cleanse all who gather in your name, so that we may ask to be a forgiven and faithful people. Where it must be, make us able to accept your judgment and help us bravely bear suffering through the example of your son Jesus Christ.

LESSON EIGHT

PURPOSE

To review the symbolic content of the Book of Revelation as a message intended to show God's power as permanent, leading toward triumph in a new world where suffering and sorrow are ended and faithful Christians enter an eternal relationship of closeness to God.

SUGGESTED PROCEDURE

Ask group members to find in their Bibles two of the best-known passages in the Book of Revelation, 21:1-7 and 22:1-5. Select a good reader to read each of these passages aloud.

At this point use Video Lesson Eight, allowing 18 minutes. Rewind the tape at the close of the lesson. Let class members know where videotapes are kept when they are not in use, so that individuals may check out this tape later for review.

Today you need to draw to a conclusion the entire eight-part video study. Remind the class members that the key question you have been using has both a personal and a corporate focus. State the question in two forms:

What message do you find in today's passage for you or for your congregation? What is the value of the entire Book of Revelation for your personal faith and for the life of your congregation?

Ask class members to find page 92 in *Breaking the Code* and see how the teaching of the Qumram sect differed from John's account in Revelation. (Victory over evil needed the military help of the faithful according to the teachings of the Qumran sect. In Revelation human help isn't needed; Christ's Word is sufficient.)

If time permits, consider these additional discussion questions:

In Romans 13:4 Paul writes about the state as God's servant. In the Book of Revelation John seems to cast the state in a different light. How would you explain the difference?

Why would John portray the glory of heaven in terms of a city?

Call upon group members each to offer a sentence prayer if that is appropriate. Or, you might offer the following prayer:

We thank you, O God, for the new insights you have given us as we have thought about the Book of Revelation. There is still much that we do not understand. The more we know the more we disagree with some of our fellow Christians. Even so, we pray that our love may increase toward them as we recognize your love reaching out to all of us. Continue to keep us growing, we pray in the name of Christ.

POINTERS FOR LEADERS: SIMULTANEOUS MESSAGES

Leander Keck, in his book *The Church Confident* (Abingdon, 1993; pages 101-103), points out how the way persons communicate bears on the Book of Revelation:

"In reading, as in writing, communication is sequential . . . one follows the text from beginning to end. . . . In viewing a painting or a piece of sculpture, however, the communication is simultaneous as the eye takes in form, line, color, and composition all at once, even if one looks at parts of the work.

"The difference becomes even more obvious when one reads a description of a work of art. Then one discovers that the sequence of words and sentences cannot communicate what strikes the eye simultaneously because one can write and read only one thing at a time. In my work as a teacher of the New Testament, repeatedly this phenomenon has frustrated my efforts to teach the Book of Revelation, where a sequence of words tries to convey what sometimes the seer saw simultaneously. . . .

"Today's technology has made it possible for the combination of sound, image, and words to communicate a quite different power. In music video, powerful rhythms and sounds merge with swiftly moving images accompanied by words in order to offer an experience of participation by resonating with the performance. In terms of communicating, the contrast between silent reading and vibrating with MTV could hardly be greater. If reading appeals to reason and reflection, MTV appeals to emotion and immediacy."

Music videos can be seen on the MTV channel, available through cable telecasting. MTV's popularity with youth and young adults often befuddles the older generation, but might well be useful in understanding Revelation. If you are not familiar with MTV, find an opportunity to watch for awhile. First, turn the sound completely off. Then increase the volume slowly.

Another example of cumulative rather than sequential communication is the three-ring circus. Lions and tigers, musicians, clowns, trapeze artists, and even hucksters selling popcorn play their parts at the same time, giving the audience a total immersion in the experience.

Can we create a similar impact with the Book of Revelation? Try reading aloud. Practice it to add dramatic changes of speed and inflection. Then read it to one or more other persons.

Revelation 1:3 tells us the author expected this Scripture to be read aloud, reaching others through the ears. There are countless paintings based on the words of John of Patmos, usually incorporating much detail. Works of art make their own impact on attempts to understand Revelation, but oral reading works much like old-time radio and allows the hearer to form pictures in the mind.

Expanding This Study
Into A Thirteen-Week Quarter

1. "An Introduction for Today"
Use Video Lesson One and Metzger, chapter 1. Browse through the entire Book of Revelation. *See pages 4-6, this guide.*

2. "The Original Introduction"
Use Revelation 1:1-20 and Metzger, chapter 2. Do not use the video this time. *See pages 4-6, this guide.*

3. "Messages to Churches"
Use Revelation 2:1-29, Video Lesson Two, and Metzger, chapter 3. *See pages 7-9, this guide.*

4. "More Messages to Churches"
Use Revelation 3:1-22 and Metzger, chapter 4. Do not use the video this time. *See pages 7-9, this guide.*

5. "God and the Lamb"
Use Revelation 4:1—5:14, Video Lesson Three, and Metzger, chapter 5. *See pages 10-11, this guide.*

6. "Seven Seals on the Scroll"
Use Revelation 6:1—8:4, Video Lesson Four, and Metzger, chapter 6. *See pages 12-14, this guide.*

7. "Seven Trumpets"
Use Revelation 8:5—11:19, Video Lesson Five, and Metzger, chapter 7. *See pages 15-16, this guide.*

8. "The Dragon and Two Beasts"
Use Revelation 12:1—13:18, Video Lesson Six, and first part of Metzger, chapter 8 as far as "Begin with the following chapter." *See pages 17-19, this guide.*

9. "The 144,000"
Use Revelation 14:1-20 and last part of Metzger, chapter 8 from "Begin with the following chapter." Do not use the video this time. *See pages 17-19, this guide.*

10. "Armageddon"

Use Revelation 15:1— 16:21, Video Lesson Seven, and first part of Metzger, chapter 9 as far as "Finally the seventh angel." *See pages 20-21, this guide.*

11. "The Mysterious Babylon"

Use Revelation 17:1—18:24 and last part of Metzger, chapter 9 beginning with "Finally the seventh angel." Do not use the video this time. *See pages 20-21, this guide.*

12. "Death and Judgment"

Use Revelation 19:1—20:15 and Metzger, chapter 10. Do not use the video this time. *See pages 22-24, this guide.*

13. "New Heaven and New Earth"

Use Revelation 21:1— 22:21, Video Lesson Eight, and Metzger, chapter 11. *See pages 22-24, this guide.*

Condensing This Study Into Four Lessons

For those classes unable to spend eight hours studying Dr. Metzger's video presentations and his book, *Breaking the Code*, four lessons will provide a brief introduction to these resources. Participants should be urged to keep up with the suggested readings from *Breaking the Code* and from the Bible.

For a four-week series, allow two video lessons each week, with brief discussion time between the two tapes.

LESSON ONE (4-WEEK PLAN)

Materials for Advance Reading: *Breaking the Code*, chapters 1—4
    Revelation 1:1—3:22

Give a brief introduction.
Use Video Lesson One.
Select an activity from pages 4-6 of this guide. Follow the activity with
    Video Lesson Two.
Discuss a question from page 8 of this guide.
Close with prayer from page 6.

LESSON TWO (4-WEEK PLAN)

Materials for Advance Reading:
    Breaking the Code, chapters 5 and 6
    Revelation 4:1—8:4

Give a brief introduction.
Use Video Lesson Three.
Select an activity from pages 10-11 of this guide.
Use Video Lesson Four.
Discuss pages 12-14 of this guide.
Close with prayer from page 14.

LESSON THREE (4-WEEK PLAN)

Materials for Advance Reading:
    Breaking the Code, chapters 7 and 8
    Revelation 8:5—14:20

Give a brief introduction.
Use Video Lesson Five.
Select an activity from pages 15-16 of this guide.
Use Video Lesson Six.
Discuss pages 18-19 of this guide.
Close with prayer from page 19.

LESSON FOUR (4-WEEK PLAN)
Materials for Advance Reading:
Breaking the Code, chapters 9—11
Revelation 15:1—22:21

Give a brief introduction.
Use Video Lesson Seven.
Select an activity from pages 20-21 of this guide.
Use Video Lesson Eight.
Discuss a question from pages 22-23 of this guide.
Close with a prayer from page 23.

FEWER THAN FOUR LESSONS
Do not attempt to show more than two video lessons at one time. (Even when two are shown, a different activity inserted between the two is recommended.)

Use Video Lesson One with a group that wants a one-time presentation.

Bibliography—
If You Want To Learn More

Various points of view are found in the books listed below. Some additional volumes are included in a list on pages 107 and 108 of *Breaking the Code.*

Barclay, William. *The Revelation of John,* 2 volumes. Philadelphia: Westminster Press, 1976. A useful commentary, primarily for lay people.

Boring, M. Eugene. *Revelation.* Louisville: Westminster John Knox Press, 1989. A volume in the series, *Interpretation, A Bible Commentary for Teaching and Preaching.*

Caird, George B. *The Revelation of St. John the Divine.* New York: Harper & Row, 1966. A standard, verse-by-verse commentary.

Clouse, Robert G., ed. *The Meaning of the Millennium.* Downers Grove, Illinois: InterVarsity Press, 1977. Four authors discuss the main views of the millennium (Revelation 20).

Ewert, David. *The Church Under Fire.* Hillsboro, Kansas: Kindred Press, 1988. A helpful and balanced exposition, with present-day applications.

Grenz, Stanley J. *The Millenial Maze: Sorting Out Evangelical Options.* Downers Grove, Illinois: InterVarsity, 1992.

Jeffrey, D.L., ed. *A Dictionary of Biblical Tradition in English Literature.* Grand Rapids, Michigan: Wm. B. Eerdmans Publishing Co., 1992. Draws connections between scenes described in Revelation and contemporary literature.

Jewett, Robert. *Jesus Against the Rapture: Seven Unexpected Prophecies.* Philadelphia: Westminster Press, 1979. A response to the perspective found in various popular books by Hal Lindsey.

Stott, John R. W. *What Christ Thinks of the Church.* Wheaton, Illinois: Shaw Publishers, 1990. Deals with Revelation 1—3.

Wainwright, Arthur. *Mysterious Apocalypse: Interpreting the Book of Revelation.* Atlanta: Abingdon Press, 1993. Contains different representations of art based on the Apocalypse.

Revelation's Seven Beatitudes

Blessed is the one who reads aloud the words of the prophecy, and blessed are those who hear and who keep what is written in it; for the time is near. (1:3)

Blessed are the dead who from now on die in the Lord. "Yes," says the Spirit, "they will rest from their labors, for their deeds from their labors, for their deeds follow them." (14:13)

Blessed is the one who stays awake and is clothed, not going about naked and exposed to shame. (16:15)

Blessed are those who are invited to the marriage supper of the lamb. (19:9)

Blessed and holy are those who share in the first resurrection. Over these the second death has no power, but they will be priests of God and of Christ, and they will reign with him a thousand years. (20:6)

Blessed is the one who keeps the words of the prophecy of this book. (22:7)

Blessed are those who wash their robes, so that they will have the right to the tree of life and may enter the city by the gates. (22:14)

Art and Photographs
Used in *Breaking the Code* Video

John on Patmos—Burgkmair, Hans the Elder (Scala/Art Resource)

Gladiators and Lion—Henri Rousseau—The Detroit Institute of Arts

Emperor Domitian—Art Resource

American Eagle—Copyright © Byron Jorjorian

Soldier/British Lion/Donkey & Elephant—Copyright © 1993
Abingdon Press

Jim Jones/David Koresh—Religious News Service

The Adoration of the Holy Lamb—(Van Eyck) Art Resource

Sun in Red Sky—Copyright © Jim Whitmer

Rainbow—Copyright © 1992 Cokesbury

Vision of Eziekel—(Raphael) Art Resource

Jesus' Entry to Jerusalem—Art Resource

The Vision of St. John—(Memling) Art Resource

Child in Somalia—Copyright © Jim Whitmer

Opening the 6th Seal—(Danby) Copyright The National Gallery of
Ireland

Red Sky and Ocean—Copyright © Jim Whitmer

Julius Ceasar—Art Resource

John on Patmos—(Bosch) State Museums, Berlin

Nazi Propaganda Poster— Art Resource

Shots of Jewish Prisoners—The National Archives and Records
Administration

The Last Judgement—(Michelangelo) Art Resource

Plains of Heaven—(John Martin) Tate Gallery, London

BREAKING THE CODE:
Understanding the Book of Revelation
LEADER'S GUIDE
by Donn Downall

Library of Congress Cataloging-in-Publication Data

Downall, Donn.
    Breaking the code : understanding the book of Revelation : leader's guide / by
Donn Downall.
        p.   cm.
    Leader's guide to the book and videotape of the same title authored by Bruce
Manning Metzger.
    ISBN 0-687-76973-6 (alk. paper)
    1. Bible. N.T. Revelation—Study and teaching. I. Metzger, Bruce Manning.
Breaking the code. II. Title.
BS2825.5.D69   1993
228'.06—dc20   93-32696
                                                                                    CIP